safe

Design Takes

On Risk

safe

Paola Antonelli

The Museum of Modern Art, New York

Published on the occasion of the exhibition *SAFE: Design Takes On Risk*, organized by Paola Antonelli, Curator, and Patricia Juncosa Vecchierini, Curatorial Assistant, Department of Architecture and Design, The Museum of Modern Art, New York, October 16, 2005–January 2, 2006
www.moma.org/safe

The exhibition is supported by Willis Group Holdings Ltd. and the Lily Auchincloss Foundation.

The accompanying educational programs are made possible by BNP Paribas.

Additional funding is provided by the Mondriaan Foundation.

Produced by the Department of Publications The Museum of Modern Art, New York

Edited by Joanne Greenspun
Designed by Amanda Washburn
Cover design by Amanda Washburn and Bonnie Ralston
Production by Christina Grillo
Printed and bound by
Oceanic Graphic Printing, Inc., China
This book is typeset in Galaxie Polaris.
The paper is 150 gsm new G. Matt Art.

Additional texts by Patricia Juncosa, Rachael Lindhagen, and Hideki Yamamoto

Library of Congress Control Number: 2005930101
ISBN: 0-87070-580-6

Published by The Museum of Modern Art,
11 West 53 Street,
New York, New York 10019-5497
www.moma.org

Distributed in the United States and Canada by D.A.P., Distributed Art Publishers, Inc., New York

Distributed outside the United States and Canada by Thames & Hudson Ltd., London

Cover: Matthias Megyeri. *Mr. Smish & Madame Buttly Razor Wire*, from the Sweet Dreams Security series. Prototype. 2003. Steel, 15 ¾ x 15 ¾" (40 x 40 cm) x desired length

Back cover and page one: butterfly image, © George D. Lepp/CORBIS

Frontispiece: Lucy Orta. Refuge Wear Intervention. East End, London. 1998. British-born, Paris-based artist Lucy Orta works on people's most basic needs, from shelter and food to human companionship and solidarity. Her most recent installation, at the 2005 Venice Biennale, is a series of vehicles and machines that are meant to filter the lagoon's water and render it drinkable.

Printed in China

contents

Foreword   Glenn D. Lowry   7

Grace Under Pressure   Paola Antonelli   8

Safety Nests   Susan Yelavich   16

Design for Destruction   Phil Patton   26

Materials for a Safer World   Marie O'Mahony   38

Design Like You Give a Damn: Interview with Cameron Sinclair   46

Shelter   58

Armor   80

Property   96

Everyday   118

Emergency   148

Awareness   174

Acknowledgments   204

Photograph Credits   207

Index of Illustrations   208

Trustees of The Museum of Modern Art   216

PLATES

SAFE: Design Takes On Risk is the first design exhibition to be shown in our new museum building since it opened in November 2004. In the tradition of such great Museum of Modern Art shows as *Machine Art* of 1934, *Modern Masks and Helmets* of 1991, and *Mutant Materials in Contemporary Design* of 1995, *SAFE* promotes a design sensibility in which an aesthetic pursuit is enriched by an appreciation of function and technology, as well as an economy of means.

This exhibition acknowledges safety as a basic human need, albeit one that fluctuates in response to environmental and social context. It understands safety as an everyday yearning, as well as a more urgent necessity when unusual and sudden dangers occur. It explores the ways in which designers can deftly address the wide range of our worries—both real and imagined—by integrating advanced technologies and innovative solutions within objects that are sensitive to users' habits and capabilities.

Truly global in reach, this exhibition comprises more than three hundred design objects and prototypes from all over the world, ranging from refugee shelters to baby strollers, from de-mining equipment to nutritional information, from solar-powered radios to protective gear for activists. The sheer breadth of object types speaks to the universality of the exhibition's theme, while each object responds to a specific and local apprehension. The range of objects addresses the fundamental importance of safety, from the personal to the societal level and across various nations and cultures.

The Museum of Modern Art has always been an advocate of good design as the foremost example of modern art's ability to permeate everyday life. This exhibition reaffirms the Museum's commitment to the analysis of contemporary design practice, as well as to the instigation of a related discourse. Paola Antonelli, Curator, Department of Architecture and Design, organized *SAFE* with the assistance of Patricia Juncosa Vecchierini, Curatorial Assistant. Their efforts have given us a show that encourages the public to understand not only how their own perceptions of safety stem largely from the objects they use on a daily basis to protect themselves, but also how designers work to mediate those perceptions through the objects they create.

Glenn D. Lowry
Director, The Museum of Modern Art

Paola Antonelli

grace under pressure

There is nothing closer to the big bang of design, to its prime reason to exist, than objects that deal with self-preservation. Created to protect body and mind from dangerous or stressful situations, convey information, promote awareness, and provide a sense of comfort and security, these objects offer not only efficiency and reliability, but also grace under pressure. Whether they are injection-molded with advanced materials or assembled with found parts and powered by a hand crank, they are arresting (fig. 2). Recently, a number of essays have appeared on the aesthetics of safety and surveillance.[1] They cite armor and the fortress as metaphors for human response in the age of guerrilla warfare and terrorism. Pressure is around every corner, and human resilience necessary for survival can be surprising. Such resilience reminds us of how powerful we can be. How safe we are depends on our perception of what is at hand to protect us. We may bristle at the exquisiteness of these morbidly attractive tools for emergency situations because we do not have any overpowering need to use them. They allow us to embrace our fears.

Safety is an instinctive need that has guided human choices throughout history. Like love, it is a universal feeling and, as such, has inspired endless analytical thinking and motivated science, literature, religion, and art. On our sleeves we wear not only our hearts but also big red panic buttons. As often happens with basic tenets of human nature, no definition of safety can be more powerful than the one each of us carries inside. In the interest of discourse, however, at least one interpretation can prove useful. The Maslow Hierarchy of Needs,[2] for example, is a five-layer model of psychological behavior, developed around the middle of the twentieth century. It places the need for safety second only to the need for food, water, shelter, warmth,

fig. 1 Anthony Dunne, Fiona Raby, and Michael Anastassiades.
Priscila Huggable Atomic Mushroom from the Design for Fragile
Personalities in Anxious Times project. Prototype. 2004

and sex. Safety here means security, stability, and freedom from fear. After safety comes the need to love and be loved, to belong in a couple, a family, a group of friends or like-minded people. Then follows self-esteem, including the longing to achieve recognition and respect; and, finally, self-actualization, which includes the desire to pursue one's talent and fulfill one's creativity. In Maslow's model, the satisfaction of one layer of needs is necessary to move on to the next. One might argue, and history has proven, that sometimes a strength in one area can help deal with a dramatic need in another—for instance, the desperate and undying solidarity of a group under duress can help the individuals survive with scant food, water, and warmth, and in conditions of extreme danger. The path of ascension toward self-actualization, and the stress on our neediness help us better understand what we are protecting and why. Maslow's hierarchy could be adopted as a basic textbook on human-centered design.

The objects selected for this volume, while not following the precise hierarchy of Maslow's thesis, relate to all sections of his theory, thus embracing all of human nature, as only design can do. They were selected because they are great designs. They all display a remarkable economy of thought and materials, achieved because of the clarity of their goals. They work well and are easy to use. When they do not work in the traditional sense of the word, they contribute a valuable commentary to our thinking about design and safety. Finally, they are beautiful and meaningful, each in a different way, and they all show the intelligence and talent of their designers. They are arranged in chapters according to what they are meant to protect, each chapter covering a wide gamut of social and economic circumstances so as to better highlight designers' approach to safety.

The plate section opens with several examples of shelters and protective objects, ranging from temporary housing for refugees and disaster victims to camouflage—a shield from pervasive surveillance—to examples of psychological protection against anxiety and stress (fig. 3). Shelter is followed by Armor, which includes several examples of objects designed to protect the body from visible and invisible threats, from shark bites to the HIV virus and the sun's rays. The third section, Property, is a survey of methods of defending our belongings, from our buildings and our purses to our individual or group identity. Section four, Everyday, includes responses to both mundane and serious problems from all over the world, from blisters caused by new shoes to the seventy-one percent of Britons over fifty who have hurt themselves trying to open product packaging,[3] to the need to filter arsenic out of water to make it drinkable in Bangladesh. It is a chapter devoted to designs that center on common sense and address the normalcy of danger. The following chapter, Emergency, is a collection of objects devised for urgent use in exceptional conditions. The closing chapter, Awareness, centers on the belief that knowledge is safety; diverse examples include medicine prescription bottles, night lights, and de-mining equipment.

For every object designed with safety in mind, there is a corresponding fear. Conversely, for almost every fear, there is at least one object designed to allay the apprehension. Fear is a powerful motor of invention. Fears are as basic as needs and as innumerable.[4] The need for clarity and

fig. 2 Freeplay Foundation and Freeplay Energy plc. Lifeline radio. 2003. Manufacturer: Freeplay Foundation. This solid and resilient radio receives AM, FM, and SW and is powered either by winding it up or by solar energy. The sale of each radio goes to subsidize the distribution of free radios to orphaned children in Africa, thus giving them access to information and education.

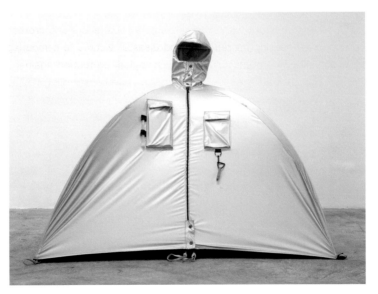

fig. 3 Lucy Orta. Refuge Wear Habitent. 1992–93. Orta's "Body Architecture" is designed for displaced people who must carry their belongings and homes with them as they migrate within or between cities.

information can be read as fear of the dark and of the unknown and unexpected. Fear of visibility can be relieved by camouflage, while fear of invisibility can be eased by reflective tape and fluorescent orange vests. Fear of disease and contagion has initiated the redesign of clothing and of personal accessories. Fear of the elements—floods, hurricanes, tsunamis, earthquakes, or fires—has informed much of the evolution of architecture and territorial planning, not to mention the design of products to address situations of danger and emergency. On the other hand, fear of not having enough water to drink or warmth to sustain life—the fear of the absence as opposed to the excessive presence of the elements—has also generated new design ideas.

The incidence of fear highlights the fact that safety is not only a physical need, but also a pervasively psychological one. In certain circumstances, fear can quickly grow into phobia. A big scare can lead to design improvements, as happened after a few episodes of "supermarket terrorism" in the United States and other parts of the world in the early 1990s. The criminals who had poisoned food by injecting toxic substances through the packaging were rendered harmless by the redesign of the same packaging.

Several objects exist that speak directly to our paranoia, such as parachutes for tall buildings, a consequence of the shock of 9/11, or lead aprons meant to protect our groin from the electromagnetic field generated by the computer on our desk. The recent argument against SUV's interestingly points to the existence of passive and active safety,[5] and shows how misguided we can be in our attempt to find safety in size and mass rather than in the agility to escape a crash by rapidly swerving a smaller, lighter car out of the way. In response to bomb scares, different cities in the world have adopted different tactics. While some have opted for unwieldy armored cans in which to dispose of trash, Paris has adopted a bemusing opposite strategy: a perfectly transparent plastic bag hanging from a steel ring allows everybody to see everything (fig. 4), creating the sort of defensible collective space hailed by Jane Jacobs in her "Eyes on the street" theory.[6]

The jungle of disclaimers and advisories that we wade through every day—about baby strollers, mattresses, gym machines, public bathroom sinks, buses and subway trains—is an example of overdisplay of protection that results in our indifference. This white noise of security is in some cases there to protect corporations, institutions, and restaurants, and is only secondarily meant for those who use such products or services. Safety can be underscored or made almost invisible. The choice is often motivated by commercial or legal reasons. The relationship between graphic design and safety is rich and straightforward. Good graphic design begets clear information. In the medical field, the recent redesign of both the medicine bottle and the prescription sticker on the bottle implemented by Target stores all over the United States, for instance, is a striking example of the importance of good—meaning not only beautiful, but also intelligent—design. In many parts of the world, certain regions of sub-Saharan Africa, for instance, but also in New York City, designers are using less-stylish, but equally effective and thus remarkable means to communicate the dangers of HIV/AIDS infection. Comics and vignettes bypass cultural resistance as well as dialects, and speak in a language that is not only understandable but also engaging.

Safety is not the same all over the world. In certain regions, what we would consider an emergency is instead an everyday occurrence. Israeli designer Ezri Tarazi (see page 166) explains that in Israel every house has a security room with a door lined with rubber to guard against chemical agents. Curiously enough, the same could be said of Switzerland and its 261,418 bomb shelters. Moreover, Tarazi continues, "Sixteen percent of Israelis have been directly exposed to terrorist attacks. I am one of them. Thirty-seven percent say a friend or family member was a witness to an attack. Seventy-six percent suffer from at least one possible symptom of exposure to terror, including extreme sadness or depression and inability to sleep. Eighty-two percent, however, express optimism about their personal future. Sixty-six percent express optimism for the state of Israel."[7]

In Italy and France, to give another example of diverse cultural attitudes toward safety, the enforcement of identity cards is considered an innocuous trade-off in the attempt to curb terrorism, a fact of life these two countries became accustomed to a long time ago. In the United States, however, the insistence on such cards is considered by many an unacceptable violation of civil rights. In Japan, walking around with a cold without wearing a surgical mask is an inexcusable violation of the unspoken rules of civilization. The fashionable response to this kind of behavior—surgical masks decorated with patterns and designers' logos, sold throughout Asia—became famous worldwide on the occasion of the SARS epidemic in 2003 (fig. 5). Resources and the economy can play a role in designing products for safety. In Cape Town, for example, the need to protect one's home can be fulfilled by remote-controlled steel gates while in Cuba discarded refrigerator grilles are reused to answer this need (fig. 6).

The idea of safety changed dramatically in the United States after September 11, 2001, and reference to this event is inevitable in an essay on products designed for security. The idea for the present exhibition began as a proposal presented to MoMA's exhibitions committee in March of 2001. It was entitled *Emergency* and it focused mainly on emergency-response equipment and tools. Because of the types of objects featured, it promised to be an awe-inspiring show on the essence of good design for real people. The show was approved and work began on it at full speed. After September 11 came the spontaneous and emotional decision to shelve the idea. However, mere mortals cannot stop ideas, especially when they acquire a life of their own on the wings of historical events. Before the end of September, the designers and colleagues who knew about the show came forth to support and continue the project. Instead of a quick-response exhibition, a team composed of New-York-based architect Gregg Pasquarelli, Rotterdam-based designer Hella Jongerius, and I began organizing a conference in 2003 in Aspen, Colorado, devoted to the theme of safety and design. Our initial proposal was to study fears, but gradually we decided to focus on safety instead. Two of the authors in this catalogue, Susan Yelavich and Cameron Sinclair, and some of the designers were among the speakers.[8] The conference helped MoMA's team fine-tune the approach and the contents of this exhibition.

One of the issues that acquired definition at that conference was the difference between safety and security. Bruce Schneier, a writer and security expert who spoke in Aspen,

fig. 4 Christian Yde Frostholm. Vigilance Propreté.
Paris litter bin. 2002. Manufacturer: Rossignol, France.
The photograph highlights the French way of urban security,
choosing transparency over armor.

fig. 5 Man wearing a "Hello Kitty" SARS mask in Beijing, April 2003

fig. 6 Ernesto Oroza. *Garden gate made from a refrigerator grille, Gibara, Cuba.*
1999. Photograph from the book *Objets Réinventés*, with Pénélope de Bozzi

provided a pragmatic and timely distinction: "Safety and security are different.... The difference is random versus directed action. Safety is being secure against random faults, against Murphy's Law...Security is much harder in that you are dealing with a malicious and intelligent adversary creating failures at the most inopportune times."[9] In his words, security is a complex system that needs to be addressed dynamically, by building into it several "security valves," and especially by allowing for human discretion and intervention.

We have come full circle to our own instincts as the best assurance against danger, and nowhere are our instincts more developed than at home, where our sense of safety and self-preservation is most acute, and where risk-taking often remains measured and cautious, usually limited to stylistic choices. It is where we are the most conservative, if not visually, at least morally. The home can be a womb, a bunker, a sanctuary, an escape, a fortress, a secluded window on the world, and the ultimate place for self-expression. There is no end to the list of possible metaphors. What they all have in common, when extrapolated from the ideal sphere that does not suffer from the wounds that our real domestic life might have inflicted upon us, is a sense of warmth, freedom, and hope. Humans will protect this treasure at all cost.

This brief digression about the home brings us to our—and designers'—relationship with risk. Risk is mankind's propelling fuel. We crave discovery, innovation, and inspiration, no matter how dangerous. The idea that displacement, sometimes even destruction, is necessary for progress can be found in many schools of thought across the centuries, from Heracleitus and the Kabbalah, all the way to Martin Heidegger. Designers are trained to balance risk-taking with protection, and to mediate between disruptive change and normalcy. They make revolutions viable, understandable, and accessible for other human beings. Good design goes hand-in-hand with personal needs, providing protection and security without sacrificing the need to innovate and invent. Good design, combined with good instinct, is our strongest assurance of progress toward a safer, more livable world.

Notes

1 A few examples include Kathy Shaskan's article "The Armored Age" in *Metropolis* (January/February 1997): 55–59; the twenty-fourth issue of *View on Colour* magazine devoted to Armour, a 2003 exhibition in Fort Asperen, The Netherlands; Francesco Bonami, Maria Luisa Frisa, and Stefano Tonchi's book *Uniform: Order and Disorder* (Milan: Charta, 2001); and Eric Howler's excellent article "Anxious Architectures: The Aesthetics of Surveillance," in *Archis*, no. 3 (2002): 9–23, which introduced, among other concepts, the awesome idea of "Paranoid Chic" style.

2 Brooklyn-born Abraham Maslow (1908–1970) established this theory to attempt an explanation of human nature, and especially neurosis, in response to other psychology theories of the first half of the twentieth century. What made him radically different from Freud and other contemporaries of Freud and Maslow is the fact that he opted to study not certified mentally ill patients, but rather such shining examples of human excellence as Albert Einstein and Eleanor Roosevelt.

3 Harper's Index, in *Harper's Magazine*, September 2004.

4 Melinda Muse included quite a few in her book *I'm Afraid, You're Afraid: 448 Things to Fear and Why* (New York: Hyperion, 2000).

5 For more information about this subject, see Malcolm Gladwell, "Big and Bad: How the S.U.V. Ran Over Automotive Safety," *The New Yorker*, January 12, 2004, pp. 28–33.

6 A sacred text of urban planning, Jane Jacobs's *The Death and Life of Great American Cities* (New York: Random House, 1961) advocated the involvement of citizens in their own protection program.

7 Ezri Tarazi, lecture at the International Design Conference in Aspen, Colorado, August 2003.

8 Among the other speakers were James Sanders, who showed, in an exclusive preview, the last episode of the PBS series on New York, produced with Ric Burns, which was devoted to the World Trade Center; scientist and prophet extraordinaire Bill Joy; inventor David Levy; Marc Sadler, designer of safety gear for sports; and security expert Bruce Schneier.

9 Schneier, who has written several books about security and has had several years of experience as a consultant, made this statement at the same conference.

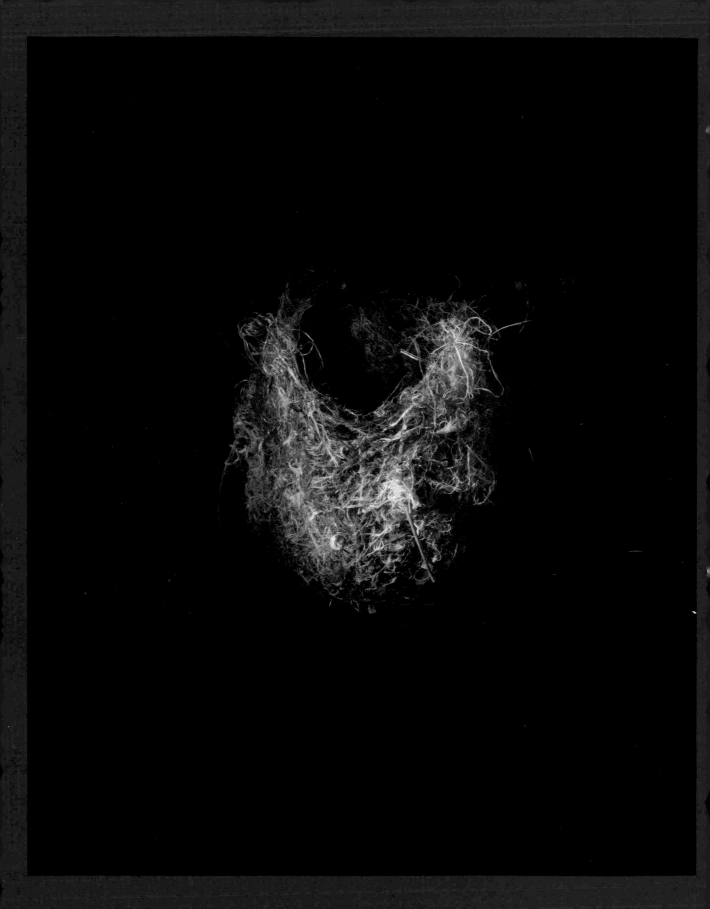

Susan Yelavich

safety nests

Fear and risk; security and freedom. It's at home—literally in the design of the house—where these emotions and states-of-being materialize. Home is where we are insulated from the world and selectively admit it. The Janus face of the house as hospitality and refuge is rooted in a primeval instinct for survival, and we build accordingly. Any consideration of the home as a safe haven must take into account the underlying archetypes and programs associated with safety and risk. These are the blueprints for our own nests, whether they fall within or outside the canon of architecture and design.

The vocabulary for protective, defensive dwellings is, unsurprisingly, by far the richest. There is the prison, the bunker, the fort, the asylum, and, of course, the womb. However, the semantics of risk are much more constrained: the stage, the tower, and the exposed nest (fig. 1). Not just constrained; in fact, confined. For in the realm of the interior, even risk is made safe, protected by the membrane of the house. No matter how transparent the walls, they still retain the powerful memory of defense against threat. So while it's possible to ascribe broad sociopolitical positions to the design polarities of safety and risk, it is far more interesting to think of the symbiotic relationship between them. Each has offered fertile territory for design invention and critique, and, in many cases, it is hard to tell the difference between the ambitions of those who would retreat and those who make claims to a brave new world.

A decade ago, in anticipation of the new millennium, the historian Michael Barkun observed the confluence of interests between the extreme right and the extreme left of the political spectrum,[1] noting that it was getting hard to tell the difference between the survivalist environmentalists and the environmental survivalists. In choosing to illustrate his point with Biosphere 2, he was more prescient than he could have imagined in 1991. What started out as an eccentric, somewhat dubious off-the-grid project, with four men and four women hermetically

fig. 1 Richard Barnes. *Icturus Galbula Parvus (Northern Oriole)*. 2000.
Iris print on Somerset Satin paper, 40 ½ x 32 ½" (102.9 x 82.6 cm).
Courtesy Henry Urbach Gallery, New York

sealed in an independent ecology, has now become a respectable extension of the Columbia University campus near the aptly named town of Oracle, Arizona.

Such coincidences of interest between the fringe and the mainstream are accelerating even faster now that the primal fascination with the arc of the dome thrives in tandem with the new capabilities of the computer to morph the box into a vortex of curves. Just as Barkun observed the commonalities between ecoterrorists and militant survivalists, in design culture we can see a strong affinity between the fantastical and the vanguard in their preoccupations with organic morphologies. They both hold out the tantalizing lure of disorientation, and both can be traced to what we think of as the safest place of all: our first piece of real estate, the womb—famously described in Woody Allen's 1972 film *Everything You Always Wanted to Know About Sex (But Were Afraid to Ask)*, as the antigravity chamber with a nine-month lease and violent eviction.

Womb

The womb has been the form of choice for iconoclasts of all persuasions, the most famous and brilliant among them being Buckminster Fuller. His 1947 Wichita House was built in a postwar flush of enthusiasm for prefabricated housing. As it happened, returning GIs didn't want to replace their barracks with something so reminiscent of a Quonset hut, however much Woody Allen might have construed it as a giant breast.

In this case, the anatomical reference is not at all gratuitous. As early as 1928, Fuller wrote of his domes: "These new homes are structured after the natural system of humans and trees with a central stem or backbone, from which all else is independently hung, utilizing gravity instead of opposing it."[2] The domes were intended to be the sole source of nurture for their residents—self-sufficient, with no connection to municipal utilities. Unfortunately, Fuller's joint venture with Beech Aircraft failed due to stiff resistance from unions that objected to the pre-installed plumbing and electricity and from the reluctance of his bankers and backers.[3]

The rhetoric around Fuller's domes—that they were dust-free, sealed with silent pneumatic doors, designed with a self-contained waste-management system—could easily be construed as science fiction. Indeed, the altruism of living light on the land has often been co-opted by those less visionary than likely to be having visions of apocalypse. Thriving on the edges of the conventional home-building industry are various and sundry dome-construction companies whose marketing strategies depend on fear of destruction from natural disasters. Fear of annihilation, however, is never far behind. The aptly named enterprise, Southern Comfort, says in its literature: "Nuclear fallout is another disaster consideration," reassuringly pointing out that "the only structure left standing near ground zero at Hiroshima was the concrete skeleton of a dome."[4] Another company, Dome Contractors, in Buffalo, Texas, bests Southern Comfort by moving the domicile underground. They advertise that their Invisible Dome Home offers "Privacy, security, and longevity, all under one roof."[5] Advertised on their Web site is an in utero fallout shelter, decorated with frescoed walls inspired by the owner's Acapulco vacation.

Faith in technology, desperation in the desert, and the survivalist's do-it-yourself ethos are not the only imperatives behind organic living. There is, of course, a rich formal history of sinuous structures that extends from the Rococo to Art Nouveau to Scandinavian modern to the so-called blob-atecture of the turn of the century, all of which aspire to a more symbiotic relationship between nature and the spaces of nurture. A more sophisticated ferroconcrete fantasy closely allied with the formal language of architecture is Javier Senosiain Aguilar's shark-shaped house for his family in Mexico City (1990; fig. 2). Emphasizing the umbilical relationship of the house to the land, he says, "With furniture integrated into the architecture, you have maximum contact with the floor, the way *campesinos* in the countryside or people in Asia do....The idea is to recline like an animal in a cave."[6] The Ur-dwelling, the natural cavity, is recovered here artificially in an odd reverberation of the organic functionalism of architects such as Erich Mendelssohn or Eero Saarinen, but with a completely different ambition. Instead of valorizing progress and speed, Aguilar champions an introverted ethos of retreat and calm. Of course, it hardly needs to be said that, with the phenomenon of Frank Gehry, biomorphic architecture is no longer cast in stone but clad in titanium, glass, zinc, and all manner of materials. Here, the impetus for invention is precisely the opposite of fear; it is spurred, in the modernist tradition, by fearless faith in technology. However, instead of using technology to express the rational, Gehry has exploited its capacity to realize the irrational, or, more accurately, to render the distinctions moot.

One of the earliest efforts to domesticate this new language appeared in Sulan Kolatan and William Mac Donald's highly publicized Ost/Kuttner Apartment (1997). The architects created what they describe as "a chimerical condition between furniture, space, and surface,"[7] embracing the house as furniture. Using software developed for animation and production design that has become the signature toolbox for so many architects from Greg Lynn to Asymptote, Kolatan and Mac Donald brought the vocabulary of the curve, which has been entirely removed from nature and inserted in an urban apartment.

fig. 2 Javier Senosiain Aguilar. Shark House,
Mexico City. 1990

Among the many antecedents that might be cited for the new digitally-driven organicism, one project in particular is especially instructive on the nature of conceptual safety and conceptual risk. It is to be found in the modest proposal for a residence designed by the architect John Johansen. The Johansen model for the Floating House (1996–97) illustrates an interesting paradox, for within its arterial spaces is a staircase—the kind called *a spina de pesci*, like the spine of a fish. These are the kinds of stairs that have no railings—that implicitly summon small acts of courage in the midst of ordinary comings and goings. While Johansen's model would seem to offer a soft place to fall should you misstep, much of the recent history of architecture has been, and continues to be, dedicated to the contrary, to removing safety nets, physically and metaphysically.

Stage

In reality, the unguarded staircase is a miniature dare in comparison with the braggadocio of the cantilevered plane. Again and again, architects have employed the horizontal plinth—preferably hovering over rocks and water, the better to advertise the risks overcome—from Frank Lloyd Wright's 1939 Fallingwater to Pierre Koenig's 1960 Stahl House, Case Study House No. 22 to Harry Siedler's 1999 Berman House, built in the Australian countryside with a balcony projecting over a ravine like a pirate's gangplank. These are our versions of the castle in the mountains, implying that entrance is arduous, but the fortress is impregnable.

Paul Rudolph's four-story penthouse tower on Beekman Place (1977) in Manhattan is by now a classical urban variant on architectural Icarus complex, testing the limits of gravity indoors. A topless living room is open to three balconies above; the topmost floor is clear plastic, viscerally conveying the drop to the story below. Marble stairs without railings, luminously lined, accentuate the vertiginous climb.

But the patent for vertigo-inducing views belongs to California's mid-century moderns, who found no shortage of optimists willing to live out on a ledge. John Lautner's Chemosphere (1960) is one of the more celebrated cases (fig. 3). Where Hollywood was once quick to remind us of the price of modernism's hubris, think of Cary Grant hanging from the cantilevered hideaway in *North by Northwest*, it was the glamour of modernism that made the risk worth taking. Danger isn't, and wasn't, the point, but exhibitionism is. The Chemosphere is not a threat or a dare, but a platform for performance.

fig. 3 John Lautner. Chemosphere, Hollywood, California. 1960. Julius Shulman Photography Archive, Getty Research Institute, Malibu, California

Any residual vertigo (or simple reluctance to be different) has all but evaporated, as "modern" sits on the shelf as one among many socially acceptable stylistic options. Today, we have the benefit of magazines like *Dwell,* which have made it their mission to relieve any lingering anxiety excited by broad expanses of plate glass and cliff-hanging houses (fig. 4). Modern has secured its G rating, safe for families and children as well as movie stars.

Until relatively recently, though, building a modern house was decidedly risky, raising neighbors' eyebrows and sometimes their ire. One of the more interesting historical examples is the 1921 Schindler house on Kings Road in Los Angeles. Rudolf Schindler designed his home as a cooperative dwelling that he and his wife, Pauline, first shared with Clyde and Marian Chace and then Richard Neutra and his family. The house was a radical manifesto—literally declared from the rooftop—a communal campsite that variously functioned as garden, summertime bedroom, and performance space. This was exhibitionism with distinct social ambitions. The flexible program was a direct reflection of the residents' alternative lifestyle, which even extended to wearing loose garments with ties instead of buttons. The irony is that the house ultimately had to accommodate an estranged marriage.

When the Schindlers divorced, communal property took on a different meaning, and the open plan retreated behind two Maginot Lines, with Pauline living in the Chace apartment, apocryphally never speaking to her husband again. It is an interesting feature of modernity—specifically urban modernity—that we have become adept at creating private space within exposed settings. Architectural historian Rosemary Bletter points out that after World War I, architects such as Bruno Taut viewed "glass architecture as the sign of a changed, international pacifist society."[8] However, it appears to have evolved less as a sign of openness than as a sign of retreat.

In 1910 Frank Lloyd Wright observed that "America . . . places a life premium upon individuality the highest possible development of the individual consistent with a harmonious whole. . . . It means lives lived in greater independence and seclusion."[9] And, indeed, glass houses, from Ludwig Mies van der Rohe's Farnsworth House (1951) to Shigeru Ban's Curtain Wall House (1995)—despite their claims to transparency—depend on the seclusion offered by their sites for elemental privacy. They share an atavistic quality, a return to mother nature, that runs parallel with organic architecture's evocation of the womb. Risk of exposure is actually quite minimal.

fig. 4   innovarchi. Gold Coast House, Reedy Creek, Gold Coast Hinterland, Australia. 2003

It is rare when an architect builds actual risk into the entity of the home, and when it happens it is universally understood as a violation of its raison d'être as a safe place. One of the most notorious examples of the second half of the twentieth century was Peter Eisenman's House VI (1972–75; fig. 5) or, as it is also known, the Frank House. The story of House VI is the story of the architect's assault on his discipline and his client, albeit one that was invited and largely uncontested.

House VI didn't take its risks by going out on a limb, by attenuating the horizontal plane—just the opposite. Eisenman says he "inverted the canon of dense center and horizontal layer of space in favor of a dense center and a vertical layer of space."[10] Kenneth Frampton called it the first postmodern house for its reprise of the European avant-garde and compared it to Gerrit Rietveld's Schröder-Schräder House—which was also a kind of polemic against the presumption of gravity.[11] Eisenman made the case for the house's palpable sense of dislocation, by claiming it was a process rather than a product.

The Frank House was resolutely antifunctional—from the slash in the bedroom floor, causing the clients to sleep in twin beds for the first fifteen years they spent weekends there—to the column that runs into the dining-room table, thwarting dinner conversation. The writer William Gass observed: "Its spaces did not flow from me as though I were their source and center. . . . The kitchen sink was a cough in the midst of a kiss. . . . The floors [did not] exist to support rugs or serve to reassure me, always, that I was *safe* on the hard and even earth."[12] Despite eliciting such poetry, Gass also noted that, "Form like justice is blind to persons."[13] And, indeed, the house had to be completely reconstructed in 1980, when leaks and structural weakness became untenable to the persons whose house it was.

But what of more literal assaults on homeowners? Of more banal fears of thieves, child snatchers, and other invaders, not to say terrorists, who make us feel unsafe? Even the royal pavilion at Katsura in Japan, which famously inspired Mies van der Rohe's exquisitely austere modernism, had its own burglar-alarm system—the famous cricket floors whose musical sound announced the footsteps of intruders to the imperial guard. Today, the privileged who choose not to employ personal bodyguards have different response mechanisms, like the one that was the silent protagonist in David Fincher's 2002 film, *The Panic Room*.

fig. 5 Peter Eisenman. House VI Fourteen Transformations (axonometric). 1972–75. Zipatone and laminated colored paper with ink on paper, each 19 ¾ x 23 ⅞" (50.2 x 60.6 cm). The Museum of Modern Art, New York. David Childs, Tracy Gardner, Barbara Jakobson, and Jeffrey P. Klein Purchase Funds

The Bunker

Self-incarceration rooms in the home can cost anywhere from fifty thousand to several hundred thousand dollars. They were already popular with celebrities, producers, directors, and CEOs of software companies and Fortune 500 companies before September 11. Not surprisingly, there has been a rash of panic-room construction since then, causing a spike in room sales as well as in requests for upgraded air-filtration systems stemming from the anthrax scare.

Some of the most famous panic rooms, the most lavish in history, were the underground bunkers commissioned by Saddam Hussein. According to CBS's *60 Minutes* program "Finding Saddam," which aired in March 2003, one such subterranean palace was spread out over twenty thousand square feet, featuring comfortable quarters for Hussein, his family, and close cohorts, purportedly stocked with enough food and water to last a year. In the end, mobility appeared the better course than perpetual internment, and the shelter became just another decoy. Infamously, Hussein resorted to literally pulling a rug over his head, in a decidedly unfurnished, undecorated hole in the ground miles from his Baghdad bunker.

Such elaborate and, it seems, largely untested plans for holding out indefinitely against aggressive intruders are not the sole perogative of dictators, CEOs, and superstars. The U.S. Congress once had its own panic room beneath the genteel Greenbriar resort hotel in West Virginia, its entrance concealed by tasteful lattice-patterned wallpaper (fig. 6). Built in 1962, it was designed to shelter 535 members of Congress for up to sixty days in the event of nuclear war.[14] Now a museum, the room is oddly prescient of our current condition, though today it is our vice president, not Congress, who takes to the bunker. Most striking, beyond the contrast of country club and military decorative protocols, is the inclusion of a broadcast room replete with a backdrop of the Capitol. The space feels prescient not only because the self-consciously designed broadcast backdrop is so much a feature of the George W. Bush administration but also because it speaks to the one thing that we want when we're locked in our panic rooms, hiding out in our bunkers, or just holed up at home: television. We want to watch.

fig. 6 Richard Barnes. Underground shelter for Congress, Greenbriar Hotel, White Sulphur Springs, West Virginia. 2003

The Prison

In March 2003 the *New York Times* reported that a couple in Virginia "spent several hundred thousand dollars on renovations and $80,000 more for wiring and all the latest equipment. They now have video screens in most rooms and a tiny camera over the crib in the baby's room. If the baby cries, the music in the networked audio system fades and the video screen tunes in."[15] And couples like this are not just protecting their infants. "People just want to feel safe in their homes," said Rocco Rutigliano, general manager of All Time Detection in Port Chester, N.Y., whose sales of security systems have jumped fifty percent since 9/11.[16] Indeed, sixty-two percent of builders surveyed for the article said they offer security systems in new homes. Parents want to make sure their latchkey children are protected along with their possesions.

Clearly, the public-private nature of contemporary life is making us schizophrenic, inducing a kind of design hypochondria. We all want to be safe from the threat of physical harm. Countless protective devices—from stop signs to flashlights to smoke alarms—are seamlessly and benignly woven into the fabric of our daily lives. But now we also want protection from those "acts of God and war" not covered by the average insurance policy. All these intrusions are simply a kinder, gentler iteration of Jeremy Bentham's Panopticon—a prison design with a central tower to give wardens 360-degree views of their prisoners while remaining invisible to them. Bentham's theory held that never knowing when you're being watched would induce self-discipline, the discipline flowing from paranoia. Today we have our Great Rooms, where parents can keep an unobtrusive eye on everyone playing inside. And when they leave, they can turn on the nanny cam.

The Nest

A more progressive and by now canonical response to the suffocation of home, in particular the suburban home, is Frank Gehry's 1978 Santa Monica House, still radical a quarter-century after it was built. Chain-link fence is woven inside and outside, its security signal muted by its decorative diamond pattern. The asphalt floor of the kitchen bleeds out into the driveway and, theoretically, onto Los Angeles' famed freeways in perhaps the most pointed, symbolic merger of public and private. Gehry famously retained large parts of the original Dutch Colonial, recovering what might have been an academic exercise in deconstruction into a synthesis of bourgeois comfort and avant-garde ambition. First and foremost his family's respite and only secondarily a public icon, Gehry's house was renovated in 1997, when his sons left the nest. The architect had no qualms about changing it, and he is now in the process of completing an entirely new house nearby.

While Gehry had the luxury of adding chain link as a metaphorical conceit, the residents of Chicago's long-neglected Archer Courts housing project (1953) recently had the luxury of removing it and its stigma. This renovation (2002) had to deal with very real security concerns. The architect, Peter Landon, stripped away the fencing that had made the building's corridors look like cell blocks and replaced it with a graceful curtain wall of frosted and clear glass. The effect of the renovation was to replace an atmosphere of danger with the aura of safety and the pleasure and dignity that come from recognizing that the space is designed, not just maintained. The residents of Archer Courts report that the rhetoric and the reconstruction are, in fact, working. Admittedly, they are working in tandem with new security locks, a buzzer system for visitors, and surveillance cameras along with amenities like e-mail facilities, a wellness center, and communal spaces.[17] This is risk tempered by both the appearance and illusion of safety. It is also a demonstration of the psychology of safety and the ability of design language to express that safeness without the infantilizing systems that society so often reverts to in moments of panic.

Our primitive instincts to freeze and flee, to hibernate or bond, to retreat or advance, are still deeply in evidence. In fact, it is still possible to identify the character traits of the contemporary home and our ambitions in the architecture of birds' nests described by Victorian naturalist Alfred Russel Wallace in 1868: "Considering the main purpose of bird's nests to be the protection of the eggs and the security and comfort of the young birds, we may group them under two primary division. . . . In the first, we place all those in which the eggs and young are hidden from sight no matter whether this is effected by an elaborate covered structure, or by depositing the eggs in some hollow tree or burrow underground. In the second, we group all in which the eggs and young and sitting bird are exposed to view, no matter whether there is the most beautifully formed nest, or none at all."[18]

Between these two archetypes, we continue to seek and build our comfort zones with risk. Whether womb or tower, bunker or spire, the job of design is to create nests people can leave as well as return to. Otherwise, we will make no culture to defend, and we will deprive ourselves of the culture we thrive on—the culture of design. If we are not to be infantilized by fearmongers, design must be understood as both shelter from danger and amulet against its inevitability. Uncertainty has its virtues: it breeds iconoclasm, opening up space for the personal, the crafted, and, most thankfully, in our paved-over world, the unpredictable.

Notes

1 Michael Barkun, "The Apocalyptic Moment: Living in a Millenarian Culture," in Susan Yelavich, ed., *The Edge of the Millennium: An International Critique of Architecture, Urban Planning, Product and Communication Design* (New York: Whitney Library of Design, an imprint of Watson-Guptill Publications, 1993), 22.

2 "Background on Fuller and Domes," The Buckminster Fuller Institute, www.bfi.org/domes.

3 Ibid.

4 "No Need to Worry about Natural Disasters," Southern Comfort Domes & Structures, Inc., www.scdomes.com/disasters.html.

5 "Underground Dome Pictures: The Invisible Dome Home," Dome Contractors, Inc., Buffalo, Texas, www.domecontractors.com/html/pictorial5.html.

6 Raul Barreneche, "In the Belly of the Beast," *Interior Design* (June 2003): 169, 174.

7 Terence Riley, *The Un-Private House* (New York: The Museum of Modern Art, 1999), 116.

8 Rosemary Haag Bletter, "Mies and Dark Transparency," in Terence Riley and Barry Bergdoll, eds., *Mies in Berlin* (New York: The Museum of Modern Art, 2001), 352.

9 Frank Lloyd Wright, "A Home in a Prairie Town," *Ladies' Home Journal* (Feb. 1901): 17, in Riley, *The Un-Private House*, 14.

10 Suzanne Frank, *Peter Eisenman's House VI: The Client's Response* (New York: Whitney Library of Design, an imprint of Watson-Guptill Publications, 1994), 21.

11 Ibid., 11.

12 Ibid., 28.

13 Ibid., 29.

14 Tom Vanderbilt, "Doomsday Rooms," *Nest* 11 (winter 2000-01): 208.

15 Lisa Guernsey, "With Wires in the Walls, the Cyberhome Hums," *New York Times*, March 27, 2003, p. F7.

16 Ibid., p. F1.

17 Gwenda Blair, "Out of the Ashes, Cinderella," *New York Times*, January 2, 2003, p. F7.

18 Alfred Russel Wallace, "A Theory of Birds' Nests: Shewing the Relation of Certain Sexual Differences of Colour in Birds to their Mode of Nidification," *Journal of Travel and Natural History* (London, 1868).

Phil Patton

design for destruction

The internal combustion engine set the rhythms of the twentieth century, argued T. S. Eliot. In its most common form, under the hood of the auto-mobile, the power of that rhythm has been punc-tuated with the warnings of horns, the screech of

brakes, the scream of tires, and the rush of wind. We continue to hear those sounds, now with twenty-first-century electronic noises added in.

The automobile used speed to conquer time and distance, dramatically changing soci-ety and culture. In the process, it also exposed the driver and passenger to dangers and risks whose conquest has become an essential part of everyday life.

The great success of the automobile lay in the astonishing flexibility and versatility it brought to life. The driver can chart a journey of his or her own choice and begin that journey at the desired moment. The economic and social benefits of this flexibility—changes in the way people work (more jobs are available to those who can drive to them), in the way they socialize, and where they live—are only partly vitiated by the side effects of that dynamic, notably, the alternate congestion and dispersal of life and space.

The automobile personalized technology's triumphs over space and time, and the agent of its triumph—speed—came with an element of risk that was, from the beginning, exciting, even titillating. Filippo Tommaso Marinetti's famed declaration, in the 1909 Futurist manifesto, that "a racing car is more beautiful than the *Victory of Samothrace*" reflected the danger and violence implicit in the speeding automobile. The joy of automotive danger appealed to filmmakers from the beginning of the medium, first in comic form.[1] Today, extended chase scenes are more often found in American films than love scenes. Near-misses, close-calls, hairbreadth escapes go back to the beginning of film, a medium where the car is almost always the star.

fig. 1 Stefan Jansson and Volvo Cars company design.
Safety Concept Car (SCC). 2001. Volvo, Sweden

In discussions of automotive safety, the automobile takes center stage, while the driver and the highway tend to be neglected. Yet the highway is arguably the most important of the three elements of the transportation system. In the United States, the country most dedicated to the automobile, driving has become increasingly safer. Between the 1920s and 2000 the number of deaths per miles driven declined dramatically, from about twenty per one hundred million miles to just over one.[2]

The strongest force in the reduction of traffic deaths was the improvement of highways. Urban and suburban freeway driving produces fewer deaths per mile than rural single-lane roads, in part, because of the lack of grade crossings. A study from the think tank The Road Information Program (TRIP) showed that during 2003 in the U.S., the death rate on rural roads was more than 2.5 times the rate for driving on all other roads. Generally, the death rate falls in countries as their road systems improve.

The second strongest factor in saving lives was the simple seat belt; all others, from curbs on drunk driving to improved tires or brakes, are statistically quite small.

When considering safety systems, safety professionals distinguish "active" from "passive." Active systems are those that are intended to avoid a crash, including more agile vehicles, improved visibility, better highways, and more skilled drivers. Passive elements include physical protection for occupants. It is these that have primarily engaged the attention of designers.

Design for Destruction

The automobile industry is the only one that proudly and dramatically advertises and markets the destruction of its products. In balletic television crash tests, in brochures with after-crash photos, in automobile-show displays of computerized collisions and sliced-through bodies, automakers revel in danger defied and ultimately danger defeated by design. Their design for safety is design for destruction.

At an auto show several years ago, Saab proudly displayed the wreckage of two of its models, locked in the embrace of a head-on collision. A slow-motion video of the collision, played on a large screen behind the wreckage, showed two cars rearing up as they struck, then settling into the positions in which visitors to the show found them. The point was that the drivers had walked away unharmed.

When the automobile was new, protection from danger inspired the simple expedients of metal grilles to cover radiators and steel-bar bumpers to protect bodies from impact with obstacles or other vehicles. In the hands of designers, these elements quickly became expressive. Along with headlights, the "eyes" of a car, they supplied a "face," suggesting a personality for the model and the brand.

These elements were often aggressive instead of protective in appearance and effect. During the 1950s, especially huge sculpted bumpers integrated with protective grilles became aggressive, heraldic displays of branded imagery. Pop psychologists read psycho-sexual meanings into their shapes. The ultimate expression of the aggressive bumper was the "Dagmars" of 1950s Cadillacs, conical bullet-shaped projections that served to dent other cars (fig. 2). The name was borrowed from a big-bosomed television actress who was famous at the time. The "seemingly Swedish" Dagmar (Virginia Ruth Egnor), who was actually from West Virginia (fig. 3), appeared on NBC television with Jack Paar and in her own show, *Dagmar's Canteen*, from 1951.

But at the very moment that the most aggressive forms of external protection appeared on American automobiles, European makers were looking at wholly different means to achieve auto safety—-automobiles designed to absorb, not inflict, punishment. The roots of design for destruction lie in the ideas of Bela Berenyi, an engineer at Mercedes, who in the late 1940s came to a key understanding: It was hopeless to attempt to create an automobile so strong it could resist the impact of crashes.[3] In fact, the stronger the body, the more the energy of a collision was transmitted to the people inside. As in the parable of the oak and the willow, in which the thicker, rigid tree is destroyed by a storm but the thinner, bending one survives, he understood that the answer lay not in a stronger structure but in a yielding one.

Berenyi invented the crumple zone. His idea was to design the vehicle to dissipate the impact of a crash before it reached the passengers by the sacrificial deformation of the car body. He created crumple zones to deform in predictable ways. The idea was patented in 1951 and was incorporated into Mercedes models beginning in 1959.

Crumple zones are now universal, but making them work in smaller cars remains a challenge. Mercedes was again the innovator with the sandwich solution applied in its small A-class vehicle in 1997. In a crash, the engine is pushed beneath the passenger compartment rather than into it. In the Smart car, the small city car originally developed by Nicolas Hayek, the Swiss innovator behind the Swatch watch, a safety cell was made visible, reassuring buyers of the safety of the vehicle.

fig. 2 Cadillac (detail showing "Dagmar" bumpers). 1955. General Motors, USA

fig. 3 "Dagmar" (Virginia Ruth Egnor). 1950

In the Nido concept, shown at the Geneva auto show in 2004, Pininfarina introduced a novel notion of how to incorporate crumple zones in a small vehicle (see page 120). In addition to the normal crumple zones, the Nido includes an internal one. The passenger compartment rides like a sort of sled on a central rail. In the event of a crash, the sled structure moves forward into a series of honeycomb metal energy absorbers that dissipate the energy of the sled's momentum. In effect, the crumple-zone system has been turned inside out. Hidden beneath sleek, shiny skins, engineering features such as crumple zones had to be pointed out by the manufacturer in advertising and displays. Other safety elements were in plain view.

Seeing Safety: Visibility

One day in 1917 Henri Matisse asked his son and driver, Pierre, to pull their car, an old Renault, off a road in France so that he could paint the scene. The result was *The Windshield, On the Road to Villacoublay* (now in the Cleveland Museum of Art; fig. 4). The painter selected a view of the road from behind the windshield. Passing traffic sent wind and vibration into the parked car, and Matisse painted with windows closed. The work is a revealing glimpse of the automobile of the time and the perspective it lent passengers. Matisse's car had a top and windows, but the closed car was still far from taken for granted. Windshields were still flat and made of conventional glass (we can see the juncture of two horizontal panes in the painting).

The horn in the Matisse vehicle was a primitive warning system operated by a rubber bulb; headlights (seen in the painting) were not yet electric. Any windshield wiper that may lurk by the hood is invisible; hand-operated wipes were developed around 1910, but not until the mid-1920s would cars have electric wipers running at steady speeds.

The painting suggests that Matisse saw the automobile as a rolling studio with windows, a room to roam, and in depicting the view through the windshield he was able to play out

fig. 4 Henri Matisse (French, 1869–1954)
The Windshield, On the Road to Villacoublay. 1917
Oil on canvas, 15 ¹⁄₁₆ x 21 ¾" (38.2 x 55.2 cm).
The Cleveland Museum of Art. Bequest of Lucia McCurdy McBride
in memory of John Harris McBride II

his familiar explorations of depth and flatness through windows and frames. The painting is best seen beside his views of studios and Riviera windows. The idea of the automobile as rolling living room was to be evoked again and again as a metaphor for comfort, but it was challenged by the needs of safety.

This need for full, 360-degree visibility for safety conditioned the evolution of the car. Headlights and taillights were joined by turn signals only fairly late, in the 1930s. Previously, signaling intention was left to mechanical turn signals or driver hand signals. "Turn signals are the facial expressions of automobiles," declared Donald Norman, the psychologist known for his interest in interfaces. But generally those expressions have been as limited as the personalities in automotive faces, from the aggressive squint of the sports car to the goggle-eyed wonder of the subcompact.

Automotive lighting provided a rich canvas for designers to express automotive style, as in the Mazda Miata taillight included in The Museum of Modern Art's *Mutant Materials in Contemporary Design* show in 1995.[4] But beyond the legal requirements for such lighting, functional improvements were few. LEDs, which illuminate more quickly and wear out more slowly than bulbs, have begun to appear. A few fractions of a second of difference in brake-light illumination can prevent an amazingly high number of rear-end collisions. Progressive brake lights, as in the 2005 version of the BMW 3 series, visually signal to other drivers whether braking is gradual or sudden.

In 2001 Volvo rolled out a Safety Concept Car, a design exploration that outlined the future of safety in terms of visibility (fig. 1). The A-pillar or front-roof support in this concept becomes a truss structure with Plexiglas "windows." The body is shaped for better vision to the rear, and the car is equipped with an electronic "blind spot" warning device to alert the driver to vehicles he or she cannot see. The car's headlights electronically "bend" to look around curves— a feature already found in a number of production models.

Another set of possibilities for automotive visibility was laid out in Ford's concept GloCar, whose creation was directed by Laurens van den Acker in 2002 (fig. 5). The entire body of the GloCar is covered with LEDs, turning it into a rolling billboard of driver intentions and even moods. The GloCar uses LED lights to change the body-panel color, intensity, and frequency according to conditions and preferences.

One goal was improving safety. Sixty percent of accidents happen at intersections at night, and higher visibility could deter them. The GloCar essentially turned the whole body of the vehicle into signaling lights. Other vehicles approaching too close to the GloCar are detected by radar, and the lighting on the panels increases in intensity, signaling the driver to keep a distance. "The GloCar projects an image of concern, safety, intelligence, and lightness, and takes the car from an aggressor to a protector," said van den Acker. "Imagine hundreds of GloCars, brightening up a city. It shows a future where cars become more intelligent and optimistic."

fig. 5 Laurens van den Acker. Glo Car. Concept. 2002.
Ford Motor Company, USA

Safe Inside

Designing the exterior of the car for safety marked the first chapter of auto-safety design. The second came with the redesign of its interior. In the 1950s, as more people drove more miles, the sheer numbers of those killed on the road rose steadily. Per-mile rates were declining, but the totals—regularly compared in the U.S. during the Cold War to the number of people lost in battle—were disturbing. Celebrity deaths by car—James Dean, Jane Mansfield—focused attention on the issue. By the 1960s, deaths rose above 40,000. In the U.S., the peak came in 1972, when some 53,000 people lost their lives.

Statistics about the nature of accidents were analyzed, and new ideas came to the fore about protecting passengers in new ways. Death by automobile accidents was widely regarded as unavoidable, and indeed carried with it an inevitable purposeless, absurdist quality appropriate to the age of anxiety and the era of Existentialism. Albert Camus himself died in a car accident. In fiction and film, from James Agee's *A Death in the Family* to Vladimir Nabokov's *Lolita*, the auto accident functioned as the latest deus ex machina. But analysis of the mechanics of crashes showed that there was much that could be done to save lives.

By the middle of the twentieth century, it was becoming clear that deaths and injuries due to collisions came largely as a result of ejection from the car or the impact of the passengers with the interior of the car. The horrors shown in driver-education courses—bodies smashed through windshields, drivers impaled on steering-wheel columns—could be avoided by redesigning wheels and dashboards and belting in passengers.

The most striking facet of the story of the seat belt is how long it took to be adopted. The seat belt was devised for aircraft, but even race-car drivers did not wear seat belts before 1960, largely, it seems, because of fear of fires.

Volvo offered simple seat belts in the early 1950s. The now familiar three-point seat belt was developed by Nils Bohlin, an aerospace engineer hired by Volvo as a safety engineer. Volvo's president, Gunnar Engellau, hired Bohlin after deciding to make safety the company's key selling point. The Nash Rambler made them available as early as 1949, and in the mid-1950s even Detroit manufacturers offered them as options. In 1959 Volvo introduced the modern shoulder-and-lap-belt combination as standard equipment. But it was the effort of consumer advocate Ralph Nader, summarized in his 1965 book *Unsafe at Any Speed*, a series of Congressional hearings, and, finally, the National Traffic and Motor Vehicle Safety Act of 1966 that pushed new designs for safety into law in the U.S. Seat belts became standard, steering wheels were designed to absorb crash energy, and dashboards were padded. Bumpers were strengthened.

The symbolic mascot of this era was the crash-test dummy, which served to humanize safety design, with a quasi-personality that asserted the automobile's triumph over dangers comparable to its triumph over space. The use of dummy figures of vinyl, foam, and steel to simulate the effects of impact on real humans was part of the move toward passenger safety in the mid-1960s.

The father of the crash-test dummy was Samuel Alderson, an engineer with a background in such subjects as missile guidance.[5] Humanlike dummies had been used in aircraft and ejection-seat testing. In 1952 Alderson began producing dummies for aerospace; in 1968 his firm, Alderson Research Laboratories, built the first dummy for automotive testing. It was called the V.I.P. Later, General Motors engineers combined elements of Alderson's dummy with those of competitive models. Called Hybrid, this dummy was gradually improved. The Hybrid III, released in 1977, is still in use; the physical performance of another dummy, the Thor, has been replicated in computer programs to predict results of crashes. Most recently, Honda developed a special dummy, called Polar II, to test new refinements to hood and bumper design aimed at protecting pedestrians.

Used in advertising, talking dummies, with voices not unlike the robot C-3PO in *Star Wars* and manners recalling Bibendum—the Michelin mascot composed of tire tubes[6]—crash-test dummies became folk figures, inspiring a cartoon show and the name of a rock-and-roll band. Like Bibendum (whose name loosely comes from the Latin for "Let's drink," suggesting the way the tires "drank up" rocks, nails, and other insults to their rubber skins), the crash-test dummy braved pain and tortures, personifying the much more abstract ability of vehicles to do the same.

The sequel to the story of the adoption of the seat belt was a revealing case study involving regulation, enforcement, and persuasion. Safety designs have necessarily reflected widely varying social environments. In Scandinavia, the same widely shared values that produce social and economic safety nets and built-in automotive safety features meant that eighty percent or more of motorists voluntarily wear seat belts. In the U. S., by contrast, the comparable figure in the 1970s was fifteen to twenty percent.

In 1974 the U.S. Federal government attempted to deal with the issue of low seat belt usage by mandating the physical design of the belts. Interlocking belts and ignition systems meant that new cars could not be started without the seat belts being closed. Citizen resistance was dramatic: some preferred to sit on closed seat belts rather than wear them. Others went to the trouble of uninstalling or bypassing the systems. The law was repealed. Designs that attached the seat belts to doors proved little more popular.

Another answer seemed to be the air bag, which automatically deployed in a crash to protect driver and passenger. Air bags were a "forced technology," as one planner describes it, whose technical potential was projected in advance by policy decisions. Regulations were imposed in anticipation of technical advances to lower costs and improve reliability. But the air bag was slow in reaching technical maturity. General Motors installed one early and very expensive system, only to find customers ignoring it. The critical breakthrough in cost and utility came with the Breed air-bag system.

Ultimately, the story of the seat belt and the air bag offers a case study of social and psychological design. The question remained how to get people to wear belts; air bags are much less effective without seat belts. "Vince and Larry," the crash-test dummy figures used in advertising, may inspire motorists to wear seat belts. They seem to be far more effective than tickets issued by police in states with mandatory seat-belt laws. (Police are unable to issue tickets in numbers sufficient to deter nonwearing.) But the system that struck the most effective balance between choice and coercion was the simple reminder chime. Ford's system, in which the chime recurs at intervals, appears to be preferable to fines or penalties.

Invisible Safety

If the development of external safety devices (bumpers and crumple zones) and internal ones (seat belts and air bags) occupied the first century in the life of the automobile, the beginning of its second century saw the arrival of revolutionary new safety features that were largely invisible to the driver. Design for safety migrated to the chip and the accelerometer and electronic brains that served as quiet co-pilots. In many ways, the new electronic aids continued a pattern that had persisted from the beginning of automotive history.

Many features designed to improve convenience and comfort also improved safety, and vice versa. Windshield wipers, defrosters, and other such items improved safety by improving driver vision. In the 1950s, as a luxury, General Motors offered "Twilight Sentinel," a system that automatically turned on the headlights in low light; today it is common.

The electric self-starter succeeded the crank starter in the 1920s. It was developed by Henry Leland, the engineer behind the Cadillac, after a friend, injured by the kickback of a starter crank, developed complications and died. The resulting convenience made it easier for women to start cars and put more of them behind the wheel.[7]

Today a host of invisible safety devices of James Bond cleverness protect us from our own deficiencies. The first to arrive were traction control and antilock-braking systems, which prevent skidding and loss of adhesion function almost without the driver knowing of them, correcting errors and compensating for miscalculations. By 2005 stability control systems prevented drivers from making maneuvers that might tip over high-center-of-gravity vehicles, from small Smart cars to large SUVs.[8] Just arriving and on the horizon are:

> **Active headlights**. Already in several models are headlamps that "bend" by electronic means as much as fifteen degrees (as a few models did mechanically in the 1950s) to follow the road ahead. Future systems might be linked to navigation units, such as reading a computer map to anticipate the course of the road ahead.

> **Smart or adaptive cruise control**. This allows the driver to follow traffic at a set distance from the vehicle ahead, cutting fatigue in freeway traffic.

> **Blind-spot warning**. When a car passes an area not covered in the mirror, this warning devices signals the driver. Volvo's Blind Spot Information System (BLIS) is the first of this type.

Crash anticipation. Radar or infrared systems enable the pretensioning of the reels of seat belts, the deployment of air bags, and even protective braking.

Pedestrian-impact protection. Draft standards for pedestrian protection in Europe have resulted in several proposals: redesigned bumpers and hoods; bumper air bags; and soft or breakaway hoods and wipers. One aspect of several proposed systems is a bumper that, in an accident, will break a pedestrian's leg cleanly, rather than causing a slow-healing compound fracture that happens with today's blunter bumpers.

GPS systems. Based on computer or, like GM's OnStar, on human operators, these systems offer safety by alerting a third party when a vehicle's air bags deploy or its driver issues a help call. New technologies can detect a driver who is growing drowsy—the chin drops or steering becomes careless—and issue wake-up signals.

Innovation in air bags. New systems detect the weight of a passenger in a seat. If there is no weight, the air bag will not deploy. A low weight, suggesting a smaller passenger, results in an appropriate deployment, different from that of a full-sized passenger, in order to protect a smaller person from being struck at the wrong spot by the bag.

By some estimates, electronic aids, collectively known as Information Technology systems, could reduce the number of collisions by one million by the year 2020, resulting in an annual economic savings of $25.6 billion. Electronic aids stand as a remedy for other problems electronics have created: notably, driver distraction. They also compensate for a decline in driver training and road maintenance.

In Europe, for instance, there is more emphasis on active safety—maneuverability of the vehicle, and training and licensing of the driver. In the U.S., where licensing is essentially a condition of employment and the primary means of personal identification, driver training is negligible. The emphasis is on passive safety—-strengthening the vehicle. In this sense, the large trucks known as sport-utility vehicles are the ultimate successors of the seat belt and air bag: steel castles that focus on individual safety in the absence of public efforts for shared safety. Their bodies suggest that they wear their crumple zones on the outside; they sport kangeroo bars and brush guards instead of Dagmars.

Like medieval knights, such vehicles bear down on pedestrians whose status is reduced to that of peasants. New designs for transportation meant that never had riding in an automobile—or aircraft or railroad train—been safer and never had walking been more dangerous. A survey completed in 2004 by the Surface Transportation Policy Project determined that, per mile, the most dangerous mode of human transportation was the oldest: walking.[9]

Notes

1 On speed, violence, film, and the automobile, see Eric Mottram, *Blood On The Nash Ambassador: Investigations in American Culture* (London: Hutchinson Radius, 1989). J. G. Ballard's novel *Crash* (1973) explores the psychology of violence and sexuality of automobile accidents.

2 For a good sketch of the history of U.S. experience, see James J. Flink, *The Automobile Age* (Cambridge, Mass.: MIT Press, 1988), 183.

3 The Dodge brothers conducted the first crash tests around 1925. Vincent Curcio, *Chrysler: The Life and Times of an Automotive Genius* (New York: Oxford University Press, 2000), 372.

4 On the Miata taillight, see Paola Antonelli, *Mutant Materials in Contemporary Design* (New York: The Museum of Modern Art, 1995), 25.

5 Margalit Fox, "Samuel Alderson, Crash-Test Dummy Inventory, Dies at 90," *New York Times*, February 18, 2005.

6 For Bibendum, see Kirk Varnedoe and Adam Gopnik, *High & Low: Modern Art and Popular Culture* (New York: The Museum of Modern Art, 1991), 244–46.

7 See Virginia Scharff, *Taking the Wheel: Women and the Coming of the Motor Age* (New York: Free Press, 1991).

8 By 2004, according to one estimate, in Germany alone electronic stability systems saved eight hundred lives annually.

9 The Surface Transportation Policy Project (STPP), a Mean Streets 2004 study released in December 2004, said that walking is "by far" the most dangerous mode of travel per mile in the U.S. and cited a fatality rate for public transit of 0.75 deaths per 100 million miles, of 1.3 in passenger cars and trucks, of 7.3 on commercial airlines, and of 20.1 for pedestrians.

Marie O'Mahony

materials for a safer world

Almost every material we encounter in our daily lives can, in the hands of the materials engineer, be used to provide some form of safety. Materials that are now commonplace were often first used in top-secret military, space, medical, or sports research labs.

Teflon, for example, began as a protective coating in the space industry before being applied to saucepans and frying pans in our kitchens. Technology's progression from industrial applications to consumer products can now take as little as five years instead of decades. Politics has played its part so that military and space agencies are actively looking for ways in which their expertise can benefit everyone. Medical industries, responding to the fact that people are living longer, are adopting a preventative attitude to health care. The sports industry has long recognized health and fitness as a lifestyle issue, with its attendant need for special products. In recent years, this industry has formalized links with the fashion industry, with designers like Yohji Yamamoto and Stella McCartney creating special products for various sportswear brands.

Not all safety products rely on high technology materials. Some operate on a perceptual level, offering protection through increased visibility or invisibility. Fluorescence and retroreflective stripes offer high visibility during day and nighttime hours, respectively. Ironically, their very omnipresence can lead to invisibility, rendering them potentially hazardous. In other sectors, notably the military, invisibility is something actively sought-after through camouflage and electronic means. The earliest recorded camouflage used in clothing was the Telo Mimetico design, introduced in Italy in 1929. It remained in use until the end of the century. In the twenty-first century, effective invisibility is possible by electronic rather than visual

fig. 1 Deep-sea hatchet fish. The hatchet fish has evolved a very effective disguise against predators. A flattened body reduces its silhouette, while the silvered sides act like a series of tiny mirrors reflecting back remnants of light from the surface of the water. Running along its underbelly is a collection of photophores (light-producing cells), which can change color to match light penetrating from above, making it difficult to spot from below.

means. This is an area of interest to those working with computers, who want to protect information, equipment, and their personal identities.

A growing range of products that we have come to regard as safe are largely based on our perception of them as protective. Health-giving fabrics that promise to secrete vitamin C onto our skin have been much publicized, but there is little scientific evidence to prove their effectiveness. Is it possible for the skin to absorb and use vitamins in this way? How much protection do we need, or are we in danger of causing greater problems by our enthusiasm for being healthy? Is a little risk unhealthy?

Designing Performance

Certain materials are readily associated with security. Metals conjure up notions of strength and, by extension, safety. Yet no one wants to be on a bridge when fatigue sets in because when metal fails, it fails spectacularly. In nature, one of the strongest materials is the abalone shell. The difference between it and man-made ceramics, which are brittle and can smash on impact, is that under stress the shell deforms like a metal. The secret is in its bricklike structure and flexible polymer that combine to deflect the formation of potential cracks. In many ways, the unassuming abalone shell offers an example to those interested in making protective materials. On the surface its visual simplicity belies great sophistication at a microscopic level.

Today, modern hybrid and composite materials are being combined to create new materials, which often result in improved performance characteristics. These materials are causing the designer and the consumer alike to reconsider materials and their ability to perform a protective function. In industry, carbon-impregnated fabrics are being coiled around chimneys, improving the ability of the concrete or brick structure to resist seismic shock. Carbon-fiber composites have become ubiquitous in the sports industry, where they provide lightweight but strong structures in everything from bicycle frames to protective helmets.

The material scientist and the engineer have become modern alchemists, taking familiar materials and stretching their capabilities, with astonishing results. Plant fibers such as hemp and straw are not generally thought to be useful in the making of products designed for performance and protection; yet researchers are making remarkable progress in using these materials as part of composite structures and are already testing prototypes in buildings and small boats. The use of these materials offers an environmental benefit over conventional glass fiber, but material engineers have yet to find a way of matching the strength of glass. But different applications require varying levels of protection so that a product that is super strong is not always necessary. A one-person canoe does not need to withstand the same impact as an articulated truck. In an age of litigation, it is all too easy to over-specify the performance needed and to forget that there are degrees of safety.

Visible, Invisible

In 2004 a group protesting against fox hunting evaded security and broke into the hallowed corridors of the British House of Commons' debating chamber. They did so wearing fluorescent jackets and, when questioned by a policeman, they simply explained they were going to inspect the electrical system. In his book *Invisible* (2005), the British photographer Stephen Gill photographed people whose clothing made them invisible. They were not wearing the latest Hussein Chalayan creation, but rather "high-visibility" jackets. These Day-Glo, fluorescent jackets, with their retroreflective stripes, are designed to protect workers night and day on roads, railway lines, and building sites (fig. 2). It is ironic that in trying to make them ultravisible, these workers are instead rendered invisible. We are so accustomed to seeing workers in these jackets that we remove them from our radar. In the photographer's own experience, if he wears a fluorescent jacket, he can move and photograph where he likes. No one pays any attention to him.

Camouflage, now being used in the commercial sector, has the exact opposite effect. While fluorescence and Day-Glo were intended to provide safety through high visibility, camouflage is intended to render people and objects invisible. But as the British military historian Tim Newark points out in *Brassey's Book of Camouflage* (1996), they also act as a statement of national identity. Some designs have official prosaic titles such as Seaweed (Chinese marine) or Scrambled Egg Sparse (Egypt), while others have been given pet names such as Paddyflage (Ireland) by collectors.

Army and Navy Surplus stores began as a source of low-cost clothing for the general public. The military and camouflage aesthetic of this clothing has been adapted by designers for use in everything from fashion and furniture to buildings and toys. In these contexts, the pattern makes the object or wearer ultravisible, standing out against the environment—whether domestic, rural, or urban. As U2 bass player Adam Clayton put it, "My interest in camouflage is based not in concealment but in exposure."

fig. 2 Construction worker wearing jacket of 3M Scotchlite reflective material. 1990. Manufacturer: Spiewak, USA

The British design label Maharishi has become synonymous with camouflage for its line of clothing but also for its accessories and toys. The company's philosophy is to emphasize the natural and artistic roots of disruptive pattern rather than its military associations (fig. 3). The company's 2004 book, *DPM Disruptive Pattern Material* (effectively, a catalogue raisonné on the subject), defines it as a "visual phenomena, whether natural or military, in which a figure is concealed by breaking up its surface with a 'crazy quilt' of shapes, making it difficult to see as a single continuous unit" (see fig. 4). The company has produced its own in-house Bonsai Forest design inspired by a Chinese watercolor; it also incorporates symbols of peace and nature. The designers focus on subverting military camouflage with peaceful and spiritual symbols in designs such as Desert Cloud and Desert Hex, both adapted from the U.S. Army's nighttime desert grid pattern.

Specially designed camouflage netting is standard equipment for the military in screening vehicles and encampments. Raffia, hessian, and, more recently, synthetic fibers have all been used to provide different forms of camouflage as a way of making military presence as discrete as possible. The ideal, of course, would be to make personnel and their vehicles invisible. In mythology, the Greek god Hades' most-valued possession was a helmet that made the wearer invisible. He loaned the helmet to other gods, including Hermes, who wore it when killing Hippolytus. An eighteenth-century shirt in the collection of the National Museum of the American Indian in New York is said to have been worn by Black Plume from the Blackfeet tribe. The shirt is highly decorated with glass beads, paint, fur, and feathers; part of the hide is pierced with a series of half-inch holes. The Blackfeet of northern Montana tell of a warrior named Big Plume who became separated from his war party in enemy territory. Legend has it that a man in a pierced shirt appeared to him in his dreams, and when the warrior returned home safely, he proceeded to make the shirt that he had seen in his vision. It is reputed that the shirt makes the wearer invisible and protects him from bullets.

In 2003 an image of an apparently invisible man, posted on the Internet, caused quite a stir. The man was wearing a hooded jacket that seemed to make him invisible, with the background

fig. 3 Maharishi. Gorscuba jackets in the reflective Fu Splinter camouflage pattern. The jackets have been photographed using a flash. Prototype. 2001-02

fig. 4 The USS Baxley, a World War I Navy freighter, was painted with this "dazzle" camouflage pattern in 1918. The design made it difficult for enemy U-boat torpedoes to determine the direction in which it was traveling. An official U.S. report at the time estimated that only one percent of its dazzle ships were lost to torpedo attack.

appearing through the garment. It was the work of Masahiko Inami of the University of Electro-Communications and Naoki Kawakami and Susumu Tachi of the University of Tokyo. They used a form of optical camouflage, setting up a real-time video camera to record the scene behind the person. The image was then projected onto the front of the jacket, which was made from a reflective material. The effect relies on the viewer standing directly in front of the "invisible" person, hence the posting of footage on the Internet. Similar technology was used to make James Bond's car invisible in the film *Die Another Day* (2002). These special effects can only operate in highly controlled environments where the viewer is manipulated and nothing is left to chance.

Real invisibility in our modern world has increasingly come to mean electronic rather than visual invisibility. This is a particular concern in military aircraft. Commercial airplanes have a rounded shape that makes them very aerodynamic. It also allows them to be picked up easily on radar. While this is good for the safety of commercial aircraft, it is not so good for military aircraft. Stealth airplanes, by contrast, are designed with completely flat surfaces; even the corners have sharp rather than rounded edges. This means that any radar that hits the aircraft will be bounced away at a random angle, avoiding the radar antenna. The surface can also be treated so that it absorbs the radar energy, thus giving extra protection. The underlying idea behind the design of this military aircraft parallels the hatchet fish, which, faced with its very survival, has evolved an ingenious way of making itself invisible in order to protect itself from predators (fig. 1).

Companies such as R&F Products in California manufacture a variety of products for radar absorption and reflection. One of their radar-reflecting composites uses an aluminized glass-fiber matting to provide protection; composite skins cured onto both sides of the absorber provide additional protection. The whole process is done using a hand lay-up technique for maximum accuracy. It is ironic that often the more high-tech the material, the greater the human input in the production process.

It is not only the military community that feels the need for electronic protection, but also the civilian. In the computer-dominated workplace, where vast amounts of data are stored, the sheer volume of equipment can cause interference with other equipment. Health problems for workers have become an issue. The traditional method of installing a shielded room system has been to use zinc-plated mild steel plates or heavy steel. These protective devices have been cumbersome to install and remove. The latest shielding systems are lighter, more flexible, and as easy to install as wallpaper.

The Belgian company, N.V. Schlegel, produces a copper-plated nonwoven material made from nylon fibers coated with metal particles that bond with the cell structure of the fiber. The result is a smooth, uniform finish, with the nonwoven material retaining its dimensional stability and its resistance to corrosion and tearing. The material is applied in much the same way as wallpaper for use on the wall, or carpet underlay for flooring. It can then be covered with conventional wall or floor covering. A French company D.L.M.I. produces a knitted fabric for similar applications. This fabric combines fiber with a range of metals, including copper, silvered copper, and copper alloys. The finished material is self-adhesive, with a removable card backing that can be peeled away. For those concerned with personal safety, LessEMF.com offers a range of lingerie online designed to protect the wearer against electromagnetic waves in the electronic environment. Designs such as the Silver Lining camisole is intended to be worn over regular underwear to protect against microwaves, computer electric fields, radar, and even television radiation.

How Safe Is Safe?

In her book titled *Fear: A Cultural History* (2005), Joanna Bourke tells how the Victorian's anxiety about being buried alive prompted the design of a coffin equipped with a breathing tube, a bell above ground so that it could be rung from below, and finally a ladder for climbing out when rescued. Before dismissing our ancestor's eccentricities, it is worth casting a dispassionate eye on some of our contemporary notions of safety.

A composite manufacturer produces a wheel hub that complies with the industry standard for safety. It looks like its metal counterpart but is lighter. Would the customer be as eager to use the wheel hub if he or she were told that it began as a piece of embroidery? A cement wall on a high-rise office block looks like its neighbors but has the potential to withstand a terrorist bomb attack. While this might be comforting for office workers to know, what if it were revealed to them that it is the tiny ceramic pellets embedded in the cement that provide the security, not the cement itself? As consumers, we become accustomed to new materials and accept the fact that in many cases they offer increased protection or other benefits that make us wonder why we made such a fuss about them in the first place. The modern soldier would be horrified if asked to swap his protective clothing, made of a textile, for a suit of armor, yet his ancestors would have been equally aghast at the notion of going into battle without chain mail.

The advent of health-giving fabrics has been eagerly awaited, and they are now widely available, particularly in sportswear and leisurewear (fig. 5). What is interesting about these

fig. 5 Scarlet in ultraviolet protective swimwear. 2001.
Manufacturer: Rival swimwear, Australia

materials is how and why people use them. One Japanese manufacturer produces a best-selling fabric in this range made from a milk-protein fiber. It has no medicinal or therapeutic benefit that the company is aware of, yet people buy it because they like the idea of it. Echoes of a bathing Cleopatra perhaps. Antibacterial finishes are becoming standard on many products, from plastic chopping boards to socks. Mountaineers are particularly keen on antibacterial underwear. Anecdotal evidence suggests that these people wear them because they do not feel the need to wash them as often as regular underwear. This use, or rather misuse, of the technology is not something that is ever likely to appear in the manufacturer's advertising slogans.

While some of the leading manufacturers of domestic refrigerators and cookers are looking at ways of coating all their products in an antimicrobial protective layer, children in Germany are being prescribed dirt pills because their environment is too clean. Medical research is now suggesting that too sterile an environment while young can leave children prone to asthma. Some parents go further and deliberately expose their children to sickness in the belief that it is less damaging to contract certain illness when very young. Hence the proliferation of pox parties in some countries in Europe, where children are deliberately brought into contact with a child suffering from chicken pox. Most of us would shudder at the notion of attending such a party, or in fact subjecting ourselves to any physical danger if it can be avoided. Our basic instinct is one of self-preservation.

Safety materials originally conceived as purely functional are now finding wider appeal in the commercial sector. Product, fashion, and sportswear designers are excited by the possibilities of these materials, which they can use for their intended purposes or subvert them for their own design. Their very nonaesthetic is becoming its own recognizable style. This love of safety is by no means new. We have always liked to sleep between crisp white cotton sheets at night or to dress in cool white cotton in the heat of summer. A large part of the appeal of these fabrics is their association with cleanliness and security. High-tech or low-tech, we want our materials to make us feel safe and protected against germs, accidents, and unforeseen or imagined disasters.

design like you give a damn

Interview with Cameron Sinclair

Cameron Sinclair is the founder of Architecture For Humanity (AFH), a non-profit organization established to promote architectural and design solutions for global, social, and humanitarian crises. Its first venture dealt with the problem of housing for refugees returning to Kosovo after the end of the Balkan conflict in 1999, when AFH hosted a design competition that drew about two hundred entries from thirty countries. More recent AFH-initiated competitions focused on mobile health clinics to combat HIV/AIDS in sub-Saharan Africa (2002), and on the rebuilding after earthquakes in Turkey and Iran in 2003/04. In collaboration with another organization, Worldchanging, AFH launched a competition to design a tsunami reconstruction effort in Asia and East Africa in 2004. One of AFH's current projects is a competition to design a soccer field/healthcare facility for young girls in Somkhele in KwaZulu-Natal, South Africa. Architecture For Humanity creates opportunities for architects and designers from around the world to help communities in need by sponsoring competitions, workshops, educational forums, and partnerships with aid organizations. *Design Like You Give A Damn: Architectural Responses to Humanitarian Crises* is the title of a book edited by Cameron Sinclair and Kate Stohr that will be published by Metropolis Books in 2006. For more information on AFH, see http://www.architectureforhumanity.org

This interview was conducted in February 2005.

Mikkel Beedholm, Mads Mandrup Hansen, and Jan Søndergaard. Mobile HIV/AIDS Health Clinic for Africa. First-place entry in the design competition sponsored by Architecture For Humanity. 2002. KHR Architects, Virum, Denmark

paola antonelli: What does safety mean to you?

cameron sinclair: I always had an interest in the idea of protection because of where I grew up in London. I could walk a mile, and I was in a beautiful neighborhood. Although people didn't earn that much more money there, the fabric of the community was built in a different way, while in the areas that I lived in—in Peckham and Camberwell—if you got on the wrong side of the street, you'd be in a tower block with no lighting. So when I was maybe fifteen or sixteen, I started getting interested in architecture, in the idea that maybe the design of spaces could make people feel safe and part of a community. I became interested in buildings that attempted that, but by the time they got built, for varying reasons they became empty shells. Like Hassan Fathy's great experiment in New Gourna, Egypt.[1] And he's certainly one of the four godfathers of modern humanitarian design.

antonelli: Who are the other three?

sinclair: I would say Fred Cuny, who wasn't an architect, but an engineer,[2] Samuel Mockbee at the Rural Studio 8, and Shigeru Ban.

antonelli: The people you mentioned have become famous for building communities rather than mere buildings or shelters. How does one go about designing for a community?

sinclair: Community is more than just about people getting on. It's about how we make our lives work together. When architects are dealing with crises, they tend to think, "Let's create something that's innovative, low-cost, long-lasting." And these are all great things to consider, but they never think about, "How do we create an economic engine in the community so people can put food on the table?" That's another idea about safety, How I can protect my family from dying of starvation?

antonelli: Architects sometimes can be very idealistic, but they cannot make their dreams happen unless they convince everybody else.

sinclair: You have to be really part of the community. The way that we [at Architecture For Humanity] have always tried to work has been as an equal partnership between the community and the designer. There was a real idealism in the sixties and seventies, but there's no such thing as utopia. No, not anymore, not since 9/11 and the acknowledgment of the danger of domestic terrorism. A whole conversation unto itself is, How have architects responded to an act of terrorism in the United States? How do you create a safe building? Do you put bollards up? Or do you follow Jane Jacobs's "Eyes on the street" idea?[3] Does a rich fabric create a safer neighborhood than putting big concrete bollards around public buildings?

There have been a lot of interesting projects that started out post–9/11. Somebody came up with the idea that they would put web cameras all along the Canada–U.S. border, and that Americans could log onto the computer and make sure that nobody was running across.

antonelli: Citizen watch, basically.

sinclair: Yes, citizen watch on a national level. It seems crazy but, in a way, I would rather have that than unmanned drones patrolling around.

antonelli: What does safety mean to people in different parts of the world?

sinclair: It's a community fabric, and it's a level of trust. No matter what laws you create or what politicians say on television to make us feel better, if you and your neighbors feel that your street is a safe street, you have a safe street. When I've traveled to developing countries, within two days, everyone knows I'm there. Because word spreads. I will stay with somebody, and they'll call their cousin, their uncle, their brother, their friends. I feel more protected traveling on my own, as there is a community looking out for me. It's the community that makes me feel safe.

antonelli: What makes an architect "humanitarian"?

sinclair: Primarily the choices that are made in order to get a project completed. The winning designs for the Mobile Health Clinic project,[4] for instance, do not look like what you imagine an AIDS clinic to look like; they do not have a big AIDS ribbon emblazoned on the side, as AIDS is still a very taboo, sensitive issue in certain parts of the world. If a place makes a point of announcing that it is an AIDS clinic, everybody in the community will assume anyone who enters has AIDS. There have been incidents where the village has moved sick people out and locked them in a separate structure. Out of sight, out of mind.

What was nice about the designs that the architects came up with is they defined the facilities as traveling community centers that happen to have medical doctors who could see you about basic medical care, but who are also trained HIV/AIDS experts. Nobody will know whether you're going to see them because you have a cough or something more serious. Some designers also introduced an economic engine, so the clinic used a sustainable model in order to be self-supportive.

antonelli: Was that something that you had worked out beforehand, in the criteria for the competition?

sinclair: Based on recommendations from medical professionals in the field, we suggested some of these ideas, but the designers were the ones who really pulled them out and developed them. Architects are essentially problem solvers. Given all the things that a designer has to take into consideration in making decisions, I actually think they would make great politicians.

With the Mobile Clinic, we created the opportunity for doctors to expand their area of response and possibly treat tens of thousands of people. Our role is not saving lives but using our expertise to give the medical profession the best possible, most innovative, resourceful way of doing that. The clinics themselves cost about fifteen to twenty thousand dollars. The average cost of a clinic in South Africa—a concrete block construction—is almost a hundred and fifty thousand. As the designs are far more cost-effective than traditional construction, this allows medical professionals to spend more of their funding on equipment, salaries, or drugs. These designs therefore could possibly save lives also because they're cost-saving. However, in order to run the clinics, you need to have trained medical professionals; you also need to make sure that if you put people on HIV drugs, they have to be on drugs for the rest of their lives, so there is a time and money commitment, and although it's only twenty thousand to build the clinic, you may need half a million dollars to make the clinic run. That was something we learned in the development process; although we created the ability to protect, in a way, there's a lot of other things that need to come into play in order for that to happen. There's an organization called Worldchanging,[5] an amazing collection of thinkers, who talk a lot about sustainable development. True sustainable development means also creating engines of growth that allow for social and economic change.

antonelli: What kind of wisdom specific to contemporary architecture and design can you bring to emergency situations?

sinclair: Especially in disaster situations, you can try to introduce leapfrog technologies. "Leapfrogging" means that rather than taking outmoded, outdated technologies and putting them into territories that never had them—i.e., like a telephone line—you bring in modern, cutting-edge technology like wireless—and incorporate it in the reconstruction process. A good example of this is that within a week of the tsunami, people had already developed SMS text-messaging as an early warning system. When the second earthquake hit Indonesia three months later, the technology was well in use.

antonelli: Can the so-called developed world learn something from the so-called developing world, in terms of preparedness?

sinclair: Well, the most glaring example, I think, actually was a personal story about a Freeplay radio that was developed for Africa (see page 11).[6] With AIDS spreading at such a fast pace, the designer, Trevor Bayliss, felt that if you had a radio that was tuned in to an educational radio station, you could educate millions of kids. You put the radio in somebody's room and bring the kids in, and that becomes a classroom. Bayliss made it solar-powered and with a wind-up crank, very low-tech, and for that reason also very forward-thinking. This radio became very, very popular throughout Africa. The Freeplay Foundation set up a system whereby consumers would buy the top-of-the-line version, and their money, with some supplemental funding, would provide the basic radio to the rural communities for free.

I have one. Two years ago, when all the lights went out in New York, I grabbed my Freeplay, cranked it up, found out what was going on, and was able to relay information to our neighbors. And, in the morning, I sat on my stoop in the sun and used solar power to listen to NPR [National Public Radio]. Before I knew it, there was a crowd of maybe forty, fifty people standing around listening to the radio. All these people stood around with their iPods and cell phones . . . but nothing could be charged. The source of information was something that came from a developing country.

antonelli: In general, what I've found in industrial design is that, because of how advanced things have become, it's very important to learn the basics in order to master complexity. Have you found the same when it comes to basic needs, what people need in order to survive and to feel safe?

sinclair: There's a big drive in the development community to mass-produce as many homes as possible, because people need homes. But people want a home that is a real place. What happens in the developing world all the time is a push for mass-customization. You can take a kit of parts and adapt it. Some of the designs that came from the Kosovo exhibit were fascinating because they played on this mass-customization. They utilized local materials and technologies, plugged them into a system that was preexisting, and introduced new technologies in order to provide clean water, energy, and a clean place to sleep, all basic life needs.

antonelli: Can you tell us more about the Kosovo competition?

sinclair: The Kosovo competition really is what started our organization. I was working as an architect in New York. I would go home every night and watch CNN, and see night-vision scenes of bombs raining down over Kosovo. We began to hear about ethnic cleansing, and there was talk of tens of thousands of refugees fleeing the country. When I was in graduate school at Bartlett,[7] my graduate thesis was looking at New York's homeless population and designing self-built, transitional, sustainable shelters. So when the conflict was unfolding in Kosovo, I started out by thinking of doing the project personally and adapting a shelter to support those who had been displaced. I called the UNHCR [United Nations High Commissioner for Refugees] and asked them if they needed architects, and was surprised to find they said, "Yes." I was twenty-three. They pointed me in the direction of some nongovernmental organizations. I realized that the problem was not the immediate needs of the refugees, but what they would need once they returned. Their country had been bombed; there was scorched earth; strangers had gone in and blown up their homes. Tens of thousands of people returning to rural areas, with nowhere to live. The moment that you step back into your country, you are known as an IDP, an Internally Displaced Person. And, at the time, the United Nations did not have the right to protect those people. So I began to focus on a low-cost five- to ten-year transitional shelter that could be put on existing land where the people used to live before being displaced, thereby bringing communities back together. They would have a place to live while they rebuilt their own homes. We should not be telling people how they should live and what they should live in. So this isn't about architects replacing housing, but rather giving people the opportunity to rebuild their homes with their own architecture, their own vernacular. And maybe introducing some new technology. The goal was to create a transitional home that could be utilized as either a secondary building or disassembled and used in another conflict.

With the help of a nongovernmental organization called War Child USA, which dealt with psychological issues of children in need and during war, I was able to get in touch with refugees in camps in Macedonia and Albania and find out what they really wanted. It was at this point that I decided the issue was far bigger than a singular response, and launched a competition.

In addition to assembling criteria based on what we learned, we put together a jury of representatives from the USAID [United States Agency for International Development], from governments, nongovernmental organizations, and architects. It was very important that we had an equal number of relief experts and designers, in order to achieve a balance between ethics and aesthetics. By the end of the jury session, those who had come in from the relief world began embracing the aesthetics of the projects, and the architects started talking about the critical needs of the people and not as much about aesthetics, realizing that both issues were equally important. Anyway, we had two hundred entries from thirty countries. The jury picked ten finalists. And we ran this entire project—the competition, the organization of the jury, and an exhibit that went to three countries—for seven hundred dollars.

antonelli: And five prototypes were built. Did the United Nations use them?

sinclair: The UN doesn't deal with internally displaced people; governments do. So, not only do you have to convince the United Nations that these are good, sustainable ideas, but you also have to convince a government that has just been ruptured by war or natural disaster that we should implement these—they're cheap or cost effective. Additionally, it is very hard to try and move beyond the immediate tent concept. Putting up a tent is the easiest solution but what many don't take into consideration is that displaced populations end up living in these "immediate" shelters for years, and in some cases decades. Some of the designers took their design under their own wing. Shigeru Ban, who had developed a version of his paper log house in Kobe prior to the competition, implemented this refined scheme in Turkey (see page 61). The design teams of Deborah Gans and Matt Jelacic, I-Beam Design, Technocraft, and Sean Godsell, through funding they personally raised, went on to build prototypes of their schemes [from the Kosovo competition]. A number of these have subsequently been exhibited, but many are still looking for seed money to develop to the next level.

We have also found solutions outside of our competitions and tried to find ways to support the designers by finding agencies and clients willing to implement their ideas. Something that's been in use are the shelters by Global Village (see page 60), And this is a three hundred and seventy dollar shelter that is built to last a year. They're a small design team in Connecticut. The house is like an IKEA flatpack that snaps together in fifteen minutes; it takes only two people. The form is very simple. It comes with a pictorial diagram, which is important because it means it can translate into any language. You could take these things apart and use them for future disasters. They're made of one hundred percent recycled paper that is high density and laminated with a coating. I can't remember the name of the coating, but basically it offers protection from water and fire, and it's windproof up to eighty-something miles an hour. Essentially it is a very simple structure that can create a temporary home. I happened to be talking with UNICEF [United Nations Children's Fund] about possibly helping in southern Sudan, and we started talking about the potential for using these structures for provider care, which we . . .

antonelli: Provider care?

sinclair: . . . which we haven't spoken about, which is aid workers—doctors who go and help. In certain situations they end up living in the tents, too. They give up their life anywhere from nine months to a couple of years. They're used to the comforts of the West, and then they go and live in a place with no sanitation. And, you know, if a doctor dies, everybody suffers. If an aid worker dies, everybody suffers. So it's vitally important to make sure that they're cared for, as well. UNICEF saw the GV unit and thought it might be ideal for housing aid workers, because it's a safe, secure place that is lockable, and they can live in this thing, and it can be put up very quickly during an emergency. Just fly them in on the same airplane that the aid workers come in on. They spend the first day just building their houses. I didn't even think about this, so ironically, here was the UN giving me another design solution for the shelter. So I talked to GV Shelters, and now we're exploring the idea.

antonelli: Maybe if there's such demand, they would cost even less.

sinclair: Absolutely. Because they can be mass-produced. Currently they are being built by Weyerhaeuser, a big paper company, so the ability to make large numbers of these units is feasible.

antonelli: What does it mean to live safely?

sinclair: Well, you want to be able to improve your life, right? But if you're constantly in a state of defense, you can't advance. So you never feel safe. And some of it, for instance, is not just about the home. Land mines are a huge issue, because they are psychological weapons. If you plant one land mine in one square mile, and a child walks on it and is blown up and dies, no one is going to walk in that square mile. So now you own that square mile. And here's a weapon that costs three dollars to produce and a thousand dollars to remove. As a defense weapon, it's one of the worst, because many nongovernmental organizations will not risk sending volunteers into areas where they may have been used. So relief groups are forced to make a conscious choice not to help people.

antonelli: What's the relationship between aesthetics and ethics? Is there something that can be salvaged about beauty?

sinclair: Absolutely. No matter what situation you find yourself in, you will always want to better your life, right? Feeling safe is more than having a structure that protects you; it is about living in a place that you feel is a home. And to truly create a home is more than just putting up four walls and a roof. It is about surrounding yourself with the things that bring a level of normalcy and comfort. For instance, one of the first things we do in refugee camps is we send them soccer balls. The idea is to introduce things that are a part of everyday life. Not only do you look after the basic needs of children, but you introduce the things that make a childhood, the things that make you enjoy life. Creating beauty is more than just making something that's attractive; it is about making something that inspires the soul and allows every person to feel that he or she is special. When you feel special, you feel safe. So if the place where you live, work, and breathe has something that makes you feel like you're not just a number, not just another refugee, not just somebody else who's just lost someone, then there is that moment when you feel inspired to say, "You know what? I can rebuild my life." And so when you go into a refugee camp, you find far more innovation than you would ever see in a place like New York City. Because people . . .

antonelli: How so? Innovation.

sinclair: . . . because people want to improve their lives, and they'll do it in any way they can. In order to create hope, people create beauty in their space as a means of survival. In refugee camps, people become really selective about the clothing that's given away. They will take the Real Madrid top, because David Beckham plays for the team. Pop culture becomes important as it signifies normalcy.

antonelli: So paradoxically, the emergency camps where you think people need water and food are instead places where people crave the most apparently *frivolous* things . . .

sinclair: Because truly responsive care goes far beyond providing a basic means of survival. If we treat every crisis as if it were a survival situation, then we end up only designing for someone to live from day to day. But if we treat it as if it's about renewal and rebirth, then we're focused on creating and generating life. This is where design should play an incredibly important role. Our sole purpose is to provide a better environment for all, whether it be for somebody from the Upper East Side or from East Africa. Using design to introduce the opportunity of rebirth into somebody's life, whether it is something that may seem frivolous or a product or structure that would help a family grow, is just as important as having each other. So the idea of a soccer ball is extremely important because in any part of the world, if you drop a soccer ball on the ground, forty kids are suddenly talking.

Notes

1 Hassan Fathy (1900–1989) was an Egyptian architect who devoted much of his career in Egypt and Greece to reinterpreting the tradition of Arab architecture to build socially conscious buildings and environments. The village of Gourna, near Luxor, is where, in the late 1960s, he tried to realize his ideals.

2 A disaster-relief specialist with extensive experience in many different countries, he disappeared in Chechnya in 1995 and was never found.

3 See Jane Jacobs, *The Death and Life of Great American Cities* (New York: Random House, 1961).

4 The competition, launched in 2003, drew 530 entries from 51 countries. The winning project, by KHRAS Architects, illustrates the opening of this interview (page 46). Other finalists were Brendan Harnett and Michelle Myers (USA), Heide Schuster and Wilfred Hofmann (Germany), and Gaston Tolila and Nicholas Gilliland (France).

5 Please see more about this organization at www.worldchanging.com

6 More information is available at www.freeplayenergy.com

7 The Barlett Faculty of the Built Environment is set within University College, London.

plates

The authors of the texts that follow are Paola Antonelli, Patricia Juncosa, Rachael Lindhagen, and Hideki Yamamoto.

This chapter takes us to the very heart of the human need for protection, both physical and psychological. From the primal necessity of a roof as a safeguard from nature's ineluctable course, to the emotional need for a cocoon or a shield to isolate and defend us from the perceived dangers of the outside world, the examples in the following pages span many narratives that differ in intensity and probability.

The first images deal with the most dire and dramatic of all situations: the forced displacement of people due to natural or man-made catastrophes, from earthquakes to genocides. In the former case, those involved are considered disaster victims; in the latter, they are refugees. While the political and bureaucratic implications are different, the plastic sheets that are provided to the encampments are the same. They are the most basic of temporary shelters. Architects are becoming more involved in the design and implementation of temporary housing by injecting comfort and respect for people's identity and emotions, while considering both cost and deployment restrictions. Every shelter, even the most basic, is not only meant to protect the body but also, ideally, the soul of a refugee. Giving refugees and disaster victims a sense of hope and pride is often as important as providing them with nourishment.

shelter

Homeless shelters, almost a rite of passage for many architecture students, are often interpreted as nomadic structures and are therefore designed to be foldable, transportable, and easy to install. Nearly always they remain romantic concepts—a means of defying authority and sometimes simply challenging reality. As such they constitute a lively field of engagement. They range from portable dwellings to clothes that can expand into wearable shelters. In many cases, they exploit the city like inventive parasites

From the other perspective, for those who already have a roof over their heads and a door that can be locked, there are still many threats to one's psychological and physical well-being, from radiation to surveillance to the intrusion of television and the Internet. In the past few years, the necessity to protect one's identity from constant surveillance has informed a growing preoccupation bordering on paranoia. People have been seeking shelters that can make them invisible without obliging them to drop out completely, Unabomber-hut style, from the world. The fear of being seen and caught manifests itself in various types of camouflage, from the archetypical graphic disguise realized today with digital technology, to the hide-and-seek game played against the ubiquitous surveillance cameras.

More than anything else, one's sense of identity is the ultimate shelter. The Boezels— toylike supports meant to help children with psychological impairments regain a sense of self (page 74)—play as important a role in our society today as the humanitarian efforts of architects and other volunteers to care not only for the physical, but also for the psychological consequences of disasters. —P. A.

UNHCR Plastic Sheeting c. 1985

United Nations High Commissioner for Refugees (est. 1950)
High-density polyethylene, 13' 1³⁄₈" x 16' 4 ⅞" (400 x 500 cm)
Manufacturer: Qingdao Gyoha Plastics Co., Ltd., China (2004)

The Office of the United Nations High Commissioner for Refugees was mandated by the United Nations General Assembly on December 15, 1950, to lead and coordinate efforts worldwide to protect refugees and resolve issues concerning them. The UNHCR, which participates in global humanitarian efforts in the wake of catastrophic natural disasters, is primarily concerned with safeguarding the rights and well-being of refugees who have fled to a foreign country or power to escape danger or persecution. Of immediate concern for these individuals and families fleeing their homelands is shelter.

The UNHCR began providing temporary emergency housing in 1985 by adapting preexisting plastic sheeting. Over the last twenty years, the design of this sheeting has changed to meet environmental and human needs. Technical experts from the UN, the UNHCR, and nongovernment agencies, along with the refugees themselves, have suggested changes—from adjusting the dimensions to reinforcing seams and adding eyelets, to improving ultraviolet protection by switching the material used to make the sheets from transparent to black, to extending the length of time the sheeting can be exposed to the elements without deteriorating. The sheeting comes in two standard sizes, 13 x 16 feet (about 4 x 5 meters) for individual houses and 13 x 164 feet (4 x 50 meters) for larger shelters or meeting areas. The sheeting is stored in warehouses around the world for deployment by the UNHCR emergency-response service within seventy-two hours of a crisis. On average, 500,000 to one million of these plastic sheets, with the boldly printed UNHCR logo, are distributed each year. —R. L.

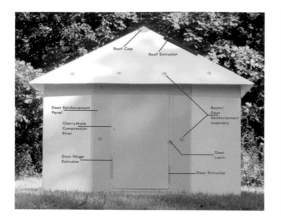

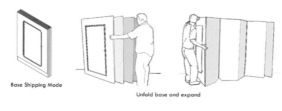

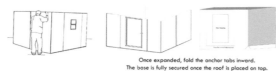

Base Shipping Mode

Unfold base and expand

Once expanded, fold the anchor tabs inward.
The base is fully secured once the roof is placed on top.

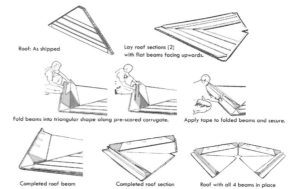

Roof: As shipped

Lay roof sections (2) with flat beams facing upwards.

Fold beams into triangular shape along pre-scored corrugate.

Apply tape to folded beams and secure.

Completed roof beam

Completed roof section

Roof with all 4 beams in place

Global Village Shelter 2001

Daniel Ferrara (American, born 1941) and **Mia Ferrara** (American, born 1977) of **Ferrara Design, Inc.** (USA, est. 1968)
Triple-wall fiberboard corrugate, 7' 5" x 8' 2½" x 8' 2½" (234 x 250 x 250 cm)
Manufacturers: Global Village Shelters, LLC, USA, in partnership with Weyerhaeuser, USA (2002)

The Global Village Shelter, a wind- and fire-resistant sturdy paper house that snaps together in fifteen minutes and lasts twelve months, gained popularity when it was used in the reconstruction of Grenada following the devastation caused by Hurricane Ivan in 2004. One of its many attributes is its easy-to-follow illustrated instructions, making it universally usable. The shelters are packed flat, cost less than three hundred dollars, and can be easily shipped anywhere in the world. They provide more security than a tent, since they can be locked from the outside or from within.

The Global Village Shelters can also be linked together to form rooms in a larger structure, thus enabling them to be used for clinics and other community needs. The designers are currently developing a sturdy, more permanent structure with higher sanitary properties that would enable it to function as a toilet. The Global Village Shelters could also be used by disaster relief workers, providing a more comfortable environment in which to work.   —R. L.

Paper Log House-Turkey 1999

Shigeru Ban (Japanese, born 1957)
Shigeru Ban Architects (Japan, est. 1985)
Paper tubes, polypropylene beer crates, sandbags, plywood, and PVC, 20 x 10 x 10' (610 x 310 x 310 cm)
Manufacturers: Shigeru Ban Architects and international volunteers (1999–2000)

These houses, made largely of cardboard tubes or "paper logs," were built in 1999 as temporary shelters for earthquake victims in Kaynasli, Turkey, a small town between Istanbul and Ankara. The designer, Shigeru Ban, is a Japanese-born, American-educated architect who has been experimenting with cardboard tubes as building material since 1989. Ban originally conceived of and built the first Paper Log Houses in 1995 in response to the need for emergency shelter for the earthquake victims of Kobe, Japan.

Simplified for easy assembly, the Paper Log House in Turkey maintains the basic features of its predecessor: the pitched roof is covered by a plastic construction sheet; the walls are made of cardboard tubes; and the foundation is built with plastic beer-bottle crates. The choice of these building elements is based on the fact that they are easily procurable almost everywhere.

Ban, however, made some adjustments to the house to meet Turkish construction standards, for example, the plan of the house measures about 10 x 20 feet (3 x 6 meters) in Kaynasli, instead of about 13 x 13 feet (4 x 4 meters) in Kobe, to match the standard size of plywood in Turkey and to accommodate a typical Turkish family, which is larger than a Japanese one. Also, unlike in Kobe, Ban stuffed the tubes with wastepaper to provide extra insulation for the colder climate of Turkey.

All the tubes, crates, and sheets were donated by Turkish and Japanese businesses. The basic components were prefabricated in Istanbul for easy assembly in Kaynasli. It took only eight to ten hours for approximately six volunteers to erect a single shelter.

Another variation of the original Paper Log House, this one with thatched roofs, was built in 2001 for the earthquake victims of Bhuji, India.

—H. Y.

**PermaNet 2.0 Long-Lasting
Insecticidal Mosquito Net** 1999

Torben Vestergaard Frandsen (Danish, born 1947),
Mikkel Vestergaard Frandsen (Danish, born 1972), and
Ole Skovmand (Danish, born 1947)
Polyester with deltamethrine (an insecticide),
6' 2 ¾" x 70 ⅞" x 59" (190 x 180 x 150 cm)
Manufacturer: Vestergaard Frandsen S.A., Switzerland
(2002)

**Zerofly Plastic Sheeting with
Incorporated Insecticide** 2001

Torben Vestergaard Frandsen (Danish, born 1947),
Mikkel Vestergaard Frandsen (Danish, born 1972), and
Ole Skovmand (Danish, born 1947)
Polyethylene with deltamethrine (an insecticide),
13' 1½" x 16' 5" (400 x 500 cm)
Manufacturer: Vestergaard Frandsen S.A., Switzerland
(2002)

Treetents 1998

Dré Wapenaar (Dutch, born 1961)
Steel, canvas, and plywood, 15 x 9' (400 x 300 cm) diam.
Manufacturer: Dré Wapenaar, The Netherlands (2005)

Originally designed for England's Road Alert Group—a group of activists who oppose the destruction of forests in order to build highways—the Treetents were meant to provide comfortable shelter for conservationists who were protecting the trees from being cut down, by allowing them to keep vigil among the branches of the targeted trees. The project was never realized, and these tents were finally sold to the Hertshoorn camping site in the Netherlands, where they are rented five months a year. They can accommodate two adults and two children each.

The artist, Dré Wapenaar, explains that the tear shape of the Treetents "naturally developed itself, when I hung a circular platform with a rope on the side of a tree. My inspiration for the shape was not the dewdrop. Form followed function." From the protection of trees from chain saws to the creation of a calm and friendly environment that makes people feel secure and intimate with nature and among themselves, Wapenaar's tents promote interaction among individuals and are a reflection on the very idea of a home.   —P. J.

TRANSPORT   ROLL-OUT AND FIXING   DEPLOYMENT   OPERATION

Desert Seal Prototype. 2004

Andreas Vogler (Swiss, born 1964) and **Arturo Vittori** (Italian, born 1970) of **Architecture and Vision** (Germany, est. 2003)
Closed-cell foam and silver-coated Mylar,
6' 10¾" x 39½" x 7' 2½" (210 x 100 x 220 cm)

Shelter from the sun and ventilation are priorities in avoiding dehydration in hot, arid regions. Desert Seal, a foldable lightweight tent, is suitable for extreme environments and makes the most of the temperature curve in such situations: during the day, cool air above ground level is forced into the tent through an opening in the top; at night the opening captures warmer air. This opening, which acts as a natural cooling system, is also used in traditional Islamic architecture for air circulation. Newly developed solar film-coated Mylar is being tested for added energy gain. Desert Seal can also be used in an Arctic environment. The fact that these tents are tall enough for a person to stand fully upright when inside adds to their usefulness, whether in a cold or warm climate.

Educated as architects and particularly interested in the impact of technology on our lives, Arturo Vittori and Andreas Vogler met at a congress of the European Space Agency and have been separately involved in space design. The study for these tents was, in fact, initiated by the European Space Agency to promote the application of inflatable technology and high-tech textile materials in extreme climates on earth. —P. J.

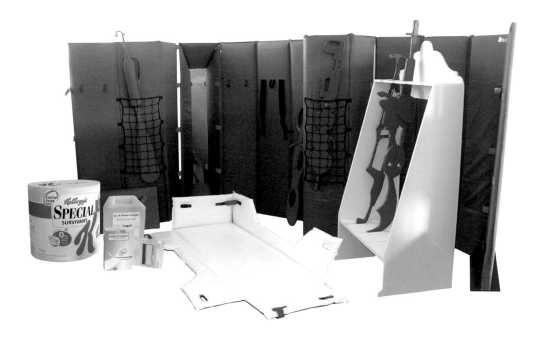

Vigilhome Prototype. 2003

Olivier Peyricot (French, born 1969)
IDSland (France, est. 2000)
Various materials
Prototype by Satellite du Musée d'Art Moderne de Paris,
France (2003)

"Because of our fears, modern comfort will be combative, in kit form, claustrophobic." —Olivier Peyricot

Vigilhome, Peyricot's interpretation of modern comfort, is a fully equipped, transportable house for the paranoid survivalist. This shelter, which withdraws into itself, isolates its occupant from the outside world and ensures basic survival needs: extra-large food packs—including Special K cereal, apple juice, and two boxes of anxiolytic pills to fight stress; five

gun-shaped toolboxes containing everyday utensils defined as today's "combat" material—a nail claw, fire extinguisher, harpoon, and rope, a socket wrench, drill, saw, level, and hammer; a frying pan, coffeepot, citrus squeezer, iron, and an egg beater; a paddle, lead weights for a belt, an oxygen tank, and a tube; an ice pick, chain saw, a Friday-the-thirteenth hockey mask, and a sword; a mattress carpet; and flexible fabric walls.

The Vigilhome was designed with a large audience and all kinds of demands in mind. It is an exaggerated solution for comfort, safety, and well-being, and a support to help one overcome paranoid perceptions of reality. Peyricot understands the contemporary dangers in progressive isolation, and translates the threat into a real battle against one's self and the outside world.   —P. J.

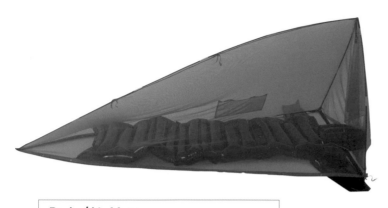

Parka/Air Mattress from the
Transformables Collection 2001

Moreno Ferrari (Italian, born 1952)
C. P. Company (Italy, est. 1975)
Polyurethane, nylon, and carbon fiber,
coat: 71⅞ x 27½" (180 x 70 cm);
mattress: 71⅞ x 27½ x 6" (180 x 70 x 15 cm)
Manufacturer: C. P. Company, Italy (2001)

Ha-Ori Shelter Prototype. 2004

Jörg Student (German, born 1976)
Royal College of Art (UK, est. 1896)
Polypropylene, 8' 9" x 13' 9" (270 x 420 cm) diam.

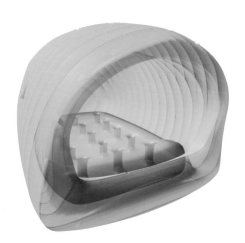

Urban Nomad Shelter inflatable homeless shelter Prototype. 2004

Cameron McNall (American, born 1956) and Damon Seeley (American, born 1976) of Electroland (USA, est. 2001) PVC with nylon-reinforced base, 7' 6" x 60" x 60" (213 x 152 x 152 cm)

*para*SITE homeless shelter 1997

Michael Rakowitz (American, born 1973)
Polyethylene, 42" x 36" x 11' (107 x 91.5 x 335 cm)
Manufacturer: Michael Rakowitz, USA (1998)

"Parasitism is described as a relationship in which a parasite temporarily or permanently exploits the energy of a host," says Michael Rakowitz in introducing his *para*SITE. This temporary and transportable shelter for the homeless is dependent on the outtake duct of a building's HVAC (heating, ventilation, and air-conditioning) system for its form and source of heat.

Following a 1997 conversation with a homeless man, Rakowitz conceived and created the *para*SITE, which was originally constructed from discardable materials such as Ziploc bags, garbage bags, and packing tape. He has since turned his design into a cottage industry, custom-making dozens of shelters that are in use in several East Coast cities.

These mobile structures cost approximately five dollars each to make and are provided free of charge. The *para*SITE is meant as a conspicuous social protest and not as a long-term solution to homelessness. Rakowitz's design has met with much controversy from residents of the cities where they have been placed, who would rather not "see" the issue. "It is very much an intervention that should become obsolete," he says. "These shelters should disappear like the problem should. In this case, the real designers are the policymakers." —R. L.

Basic House Prototype. 1999

Martín Ruiz de Azúa (Spanish, born 1965)
Polyester, 6' 6 ¾" x 6' 6 ¾" x 6' 6 ¾"
(200 x 200 x 200 cm)

Final Home 44-pocket parka 1994

Kosuke Tsumura (Japanese, born 1959)
Nylon, 43 ¼ x 23 ⅝" (110 x 60 cm)
Manufacturer: A-net, Inc., Japan (1994)

Final Home Bear 1994

Kosuke Tsumura (Japanese, born 1959)
Nylon, 13 ⅜ x 7 1/16" (34 x 18 cm)
Manufacturer: A-net, Inc., Japan (1994)

Contrary to what the title, Final Home, may suggest, this forty-four-pocket parka, designed by Kosuke Tsumura, is a wearable shelter. His parka is like a tent to a nomad. The word "final" here means "ultimate."

Tsumura, a Japanese fashion designer, has turned his eye to what most designers don't look at: the space between the outer layer and the lining of a jacket. He has subdivided this space into forty-four pockets at the front, the back, and in the sleeves. Designed as shelter, these pockets can store food, medicine, and tools, and if the weather gets colder, the pockets can be stuffed with newspaper or any other insulating materials, just as you might insulate the space between the interior and exterior walls of a house.

All the pockets are equally sized so as to accommodate the optional Final Home down cushions, which can transform the parka into an instant down jacket. The parka can be made to suit any body type by simply stuffing certain pockets with extra materials to provide a tighter fit. The Final Home Bear, a stuffed animal, can be stashed into one of the pockets as insulation or can be used as a snugly companion.

The Final Home forty-four-pocket parka is considered survival gear. If customers no longer need the parkas, they are encouraged to return them to the shops where they were purchased. They will then be sent to appropriate nongovernmental organizations that then distribute the used parkas to refugees and disaster victims.   —H. Y.

No TV Today and No PC Today, TV and PC parasites 1999

matali crasset (French, born 1965)
Silicone, 11¾ x 11¾ x ⅝" (30 x 30 x 1.5 cm)
Manufacturer: Lieu Commun, France (1999)

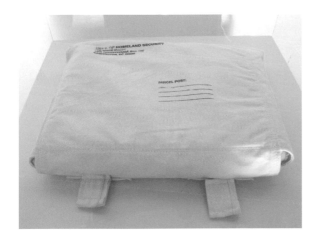

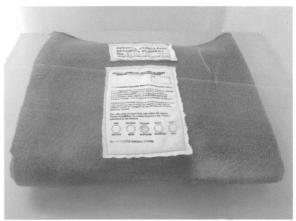

Homeland Security Blanket

Prototype. 2002

Amy Franceschini (American born 1970) and
Michael Swaine (American born 1971) of
Futurefarmers (USA, est. 1995)
Canvas, ink, and wool, 2 x 18 x 4" (5 x 46 x 1.5 cm)

Electro-draught Excluder from the
Placebo project Prototype. 2000

Anthony Dunne (British, born 1964) and
Fiona Raby (British, born 1963)
MDF, electrically conductive foam, and stainless steel,
19 ¾ x 19 ¾ x 4" (50 x 50 x 10 cm)

Hide Away Furniture from the Design
for Fragile Personalities in Anxious Times
project Prototype. 2004

Anthony Dunne (British, born 1964), **Fiona Raby**
(British, born 1963), and **Michael Anastassiades**
(Cypriot, born 1967)
English oak and felt, 27 ½ x 28 ⅜ x 70 ⅞"
(70 x 72 x 180 cm); floor: 8' 2 ½" x 6' 6 ¾" (250 x 200 cm)

Faraday Chair from the **Hertzian Tales project** Prototype. 1996

Anthony Dunne (British, born 1964) and
Fiona Raby (British, born 1963)
Perspex and steel, 27 ½ x 27 ½ x 48 ⅜"
(70 x 70 x 123 cm)

The work of Anthony Dunne and Fiona Raby seeks to stimulate the debate about the social, cultural, and ethical impact of emerging pervasive technologies. Most of their pieces pose questions rather than provide answers, and their main collaborators and clients range from cultural institutions to industrial research laboratories. The products themselves—in most cases furniture—are the medium for this exploration, a mirror that amplifies the designers' vision.

Designs for Fragile Personalities in Anxious Times (2004) is a collection of products designed in collaboration with Michael Anastassiades, who is also keen on exploring the psychological connections between objects and their users. Taking therapy as a cultural phenomenon and design as a form of escapism, each of the three original pieces of Hide Away Furniture, one of which is shown here, opens in a different way without affecting the objects that might be placed on their surfaces. These furnishings merge with the floor and the surroundings, hiding the user and even letting him disappear. Each piece requires the adoption of a specific position,

for instance, on the opposite page, a reclining pose reminiscent of Goya's *Maja*, far removed from the fetal position that is the expression of one's vulnerability.

Placebo project is a collection of eight pieces of furniture that explores mental well-being and alerts their owners to the presence of domestic electromagnetic fields. The Electro-draught Excluder (opposite) uses conductive foam to deflect stray waves and to create a shield from radiation. The eight prototypes were "adopted" by volunteers around London, who kept them in their homes for two months. The whole process was documented in collaboration with photographer Jason Evans, who compiled the results in *Design Noir: The Secret Life of Electronic Objects* (2001), a guidebook to the invisible landscape shaped by electromagnetic forces.

An earlier design included in Dunne and Raby's Hertzian Tales (1999), the Faraday Chair is a minimum yet ultimate shelter from the hidden electromagnetic fields that surround us everywhere. As electronic devices invade our houses, wave-free spaces may be our only refuge. —P. J.

zHumanoyd (baby) (far left) 2004
Tummy (warm belly monkey) (left) 2001
Hingeling (music bird) (above) Prototype
2001, from the **Boezels collection**

Twan Verdonck (Dutch, born 1979)
Neo Human Toys (The Netherlands, est. 2003)

zHumanoyd: mirror foil, cotton, eucalypthus, and roses,
14 ⅛ x 9 ⅞ x 3 ½" (36 x 25 x 9 cm)

Tummy: fake fur, cotton, and cherry stones,
23 ⅝ x 18 ⅞ x 8 ⅝" (60 x 48 x 22 cm)
(both) Manufacturer: De Wisselstroom, The Netherlands
(2005)

Hingeling: polyurethane, rope, and music box,
7 ⅞ x 12 ¼ x 6 ¼" (20 x 31 x 16 cm)
Prototype by Twan and Frans Verdonck, The Netherlands
(2001)

The Boezels are a series of seventeen fuzzy human or animal-like toys designed according to the principles of the *snoezelen* therapy, and are targeted to mentally-challenged people. *Snoezelen* is a contraction of the Dutch words *snuffelen*, meaning "to seek out" or "explore," and *doezelen*, "to relax." The therapy was developed in the 1970s by two Dutch therapists, Jan Hulsegge and Ad Verheul, and is based on sensory stimulation in a controlled ambience in order to help the learning process and reduce anxiety.

Each Boezel has unique characteristics that appeal to at least one of the senses. Tummy, which has contents that can be heated in a microwave, rolls around the neck and keeps your belly warm. zHumanoyd is an abstract baby with a special scent and a mirror in which a child can recognize himself. Hingeling, a musical bird that the designer created with his father, sings when a worm is pulled out of its

mouth. The Boezels can be hugged and cuddled or wrapped around the body to let them cuddle you, encouraging a strong feeling of physical contact.

Mentally-challenged people, especially children, are the recipients of these toys, but they also participate in their creation. Verdonck collaborates with a workshop of people with mental impairments in the daycare center De Wisselstroom in the Netherlands. Suitable for all children, these abstract objects leave room for the imagination: they may be transformed into a wide range of characters that increases with individual interpretation, opening up countless possibilities for narrative.

The Boezels began in 2001 as a graduation project at the Design Academy Eindhoven. The enormous response and demand encouraged Verdonck to improve the toys so that they could be produced at their unique workshop instead of at a typical factory.

—P. J.

Cries and Whispers 2003

Hill Jephson Robb (Scottish, born 1970)
Wool, 40 x 59" (100 x 150 cm) diam.

After designer Hill Jephson Robb's young sister lost her fight against cancer, leaving behind a seven-month-old daughter, the designer attempted to restore the feeling of security that the child felt with her mother. "I looked to establish where and when a child was more protected by her mother and how animals best protected their young." He concluded that the safest place for a child was the womb, just as for baby chicks it is the nest.

Cries and Whispers has been designed as a safe space of security and comfort, both physical and emotional, for a child whose mother is absent. The entrance to the piece, like the entrance to a nest, enlarges in size as the child grows. Cries and Whispers is a safe place to which a child can always return.

The material used is felt, and the womb is created by wrapping, wetting, and rolling it. This in itself proved to be a very comforting and cathartic process for the designer. Robb's work appeals to the emotional and the spiritual, in the belief that design must contribute to survival and focus on healing both the individual and the world. —P. J.

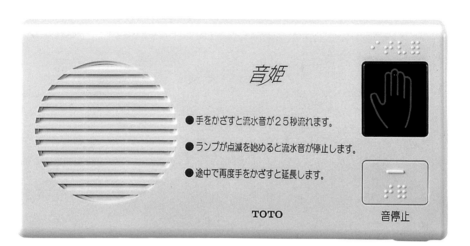

音姫

●手をかざすと流水音が25秒流れます。

●ランプが点滅を始めると流水音が停止します。

●途中で再度手をかざすと延長します。

TOTO

音停止

Otohime YES300D artificial
sound machine for the bathroom 1988

Suzue Endo (Japanese, born 1953) and
Yasushi Takahashi (Japanese, born 1970)
ABS resin, 7 ⅞ x 4 x 1¼" (20 x 10 x 3.1 cm)
Manufacturer: TOTO, Ltd., Japan (2003)

The leading Japanese manufacturer of toilets, TOTO, produces an electronic device called Otohime that solves a rather delicate problem: Japanese women do not like other people to hear them going to the bathroom. The traditional way they skirt this issue is by flushing the toilet a couple of times as they use it. That conveniently drowns out any embarrassing noises, but also wastes a lot of water.

In 1978, during a serious drought in the province of Fukuoka, where the company's headquarters are located, a female employee of TOTO, Suzue Endo, noticed this problem, but it was not until ten years later that the Otohime was put in production.

Meaning "princess of sound" in Japanese, the Otohime simulates the sound of a toilet flushing. The device is about twice the size of an average television remote control and is attached inside the bathroom stall, either near or built into the toilet-paper holder.

The device is activated by placing one's hand close to the sensor, which emits a digitally recorded sound of a flushing toilet at eighty decibels (about as loud as a vacuum cleaner) for twenty-five seconds. To make the user feel secure, the time remaining is indicated by progressively shorter intervals of the flashing green LED light. If more flushing sound is needed, the time can be extended by placing the hand close to the sensor again before the time expires.

One study conducted later at a woman's college in Tokyo found that the installation of Otohime in four hundred female bathroom stalls reduced the annual usage of water by 43.1 percent, which resulted in more than $190,000 in savings.   —H. Y.

MultiCam Multi-Environment
Camouflage 2003

Caleb Crye (American, born 1975), Eric Fehlberg (Canadian, born 1976), Karen Chen (Taiwanese, born 1977), and Gregg Thomson (American, born 1976) of Crye Associates (USA, est. 2000)
Dyed nylon and cotton
Manufacturer: Crye Precision, USA (2003)

The MultiCam pattern is a Multi-Environment Camouflage system developed by Brooklyn-based Crye Precision in cooperation with the U.S. Army Natick Soldier Center. Observing that U.S. forces deployed with traditional camouflage needed uniforms that could be adapted to any environment—desert, mountain, or jungle, for example—Crye Precision created standardized military camouflage that comes in one pattern and color and is suitable for use anywhere. By exploiting optical illusions and high-resolution digital-fades from one color to another, the uniforms make detection more difficult than with traditional camouflage. The base color of the MultiCam is more neutral than that found in deserts or woodlands, and the pattern itself is subtle enough to reflect the shades of the surrounding area, thus allowing it to be adaptable to multiple environments, seasons, elevations, and light conditions.   —R. L.

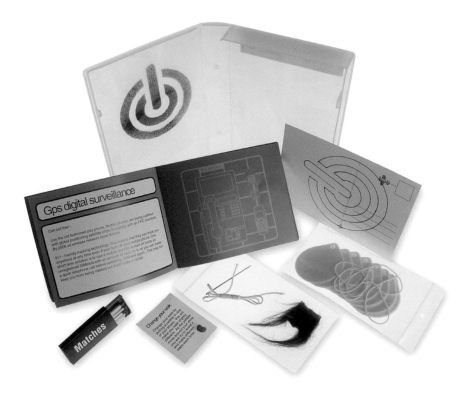

How to Disappear kit and vending machine 2004

Designskolen Kolding (Denmark, est. 1967)
Luca Leo Funch Dyrvang (Danish, born 1980), **Louise
Rosenkrans** (Danish, born 1979), **Lars Lyngstadaas**
(Norwegian, born 1972), **Kim Meier** (Danish born 1974),
Morten Just Hansen (Danish born 1980), and **Anne Mette
Karsted Poulsen** (Danish, born 1980)
Instructors: **Poul Allan Bruun** (Danish, born 1948) and
Barnabas Wetton (British, born 1962)
Plastic, paper, matches, thread, stone, string, and reflectors.
How to Disappear kit (casing): 7 ⅝ x 4 ⅞ x 1 ⅛"
(19.4 x 12.3 x 2.9 cm); vending machine: 55 ½ x 15 ⅜ x 9 ⅝"
(141 x 39 x 24 cm)
Manufacturer: Designskolen Kolding, Denmark (2004)

In the present Information Age, individual data about us are constantly being gathered, processed, and stored, and our knowledge of what is being recorded or for what purpose is often scant.

How to Disappear is the result of an interdisciplinary workshop on the theme of propaganda and manipulation organized by the Institute of Industrial Design and Interactive Media, Designskolen Kolding, in Denmark. The kit, developed by students at the Designskolen Kolding, can be purchased from vending machines located on Danish street corners. Inside an anonymous videocassette case, the buyer will find a booklet with instructions and practical guidelines on how to dodge surveillance in public places, along with a selection of "disappearance gadgets" that will help hide one's identity: a stencil postcard to mark surveillance-free spots on the pavement—all the signs together will outline safe routes through the city; a pebble to place in a shoe with the intention of modifying your gait so that a camera tracking your motion cannot recognize you; matches to destroy any evidence that might reveal your identity; a fake beard; and a do-it-yourself reflector mask to block out your facial features when the camera takes a photograph. At once humorous and critical, the kit urges the user not to disappear but rather to take an active role in a social debate.

—P. J.

To be safe, we need protection from many threats, such as the sun, the wind, insects, oyster knives, acids, bacteria, computer hackers, bullets, police batons, punches, bombs, and bad luck, to name just a few of the curveballs that life can throw our way. Armor, which is meant to protect us from these things, can be imperceptible or massive and unwieldy. Most examples of extreme protection are wondrous in the way they visually foretell the intensity of danger—think of a shark suit, for instance, or of a bullet-resistant face mask. Armor of all kinds has historically embodied both craftsmanship and symbolism. To hide the admission of weakness that is exposed by their presence, armor worn by soldiers has been designed not only to protect, but also to project intimidating signs of superiority, whether technical, spiritual, or physical.

Clothes and accessories were at first a means of protection from the elements. However, a hunter also wore the skin of a beast he had killed as a sign of his might and superiority. Today, such might and superiority have become financial; when we purchase an expensive, heavily advertised jacket, we may be doing it as a status symbol or to show our desire to belong or to challenge our friends. The path from the hunter to the contemporary consumer is not that far removed. Today, the simple need for protection has mutated into the complex universe we call fashion.

armor

Protective garments and accessories, however, rely mainly on materials that allow them to perform as thicker skins or outer shells of the human body. The difference between ordinary sunglasses and laser-protection eyewear lies in the materials used, as does the difference between common rain boots and acid-resistant overshoes. Depending on the type of protection needed, engineers and designers today have a whole range of customized combinations of materials at their disposal. Advances in technology have opened up many composite possibilities, especially with the introduction of insulating gels, fiber composites, and new fibers such as Kevlar or Gore-tex. This progress has made armor lighter and more flexible, hence allowing for more freedom of movement and agility, an important feature when a rapid escape becomes necessary in case of an emergency. Moreover, the possibility of infusing chemical properties in the materials themselves has brought about antibacterial and SPF fabrics, to name just a few of the many areas of innovation.

Nearly every man-made armor can be compared to an example found in nature—the shell of an insect, for instance, or the fur of a mountain animal. New materials bring us closer than ever before to the efficiency of nature, although in some cases the protection we crave is from self-inflicted dangers, like the hole in the ozone layer. Safety lies in the balance between protection and prevention. —P. A.

Bullet-Resistant Mask 1983

Stephen Armellino (American, born 1955)
Kevlar and polyester resin, 11 x 6 ¾ x 3 ¾"
(28 x 17.1 x 9.5 cm)
Manufacturer: U.S. Armor Corporation, USA (1984)

Giro Atmos bicycle helmet 2003

Greg Marting (American, born 1960)
Polystyrene, polycarbonate, carbon composite,
and nylon, 11 x 8 ¼ x 6 ⅜" (28 x 21 x 16 cm)
Manufacturer: Giro Sport Design, Inc., a division of
Bell Sports, Inc., USA (2004)

Face Guard 2003

Yasuo Kuroki (Japanese, born 1932)
Polycarbonate, 5 ½ x 8 ¼ x 4 ¾" (14 x 21 x 12 cm)
Manufacturer: Nanwa Co., Ltd., Japan (2004)

Headscarf 2003

Galya Rosenfeld (Israeli, born USA 1977)
**Industrial Design Department, Bezalel Academy
of Art and Design** (Israel, est. 1906)
Stainless steel, 33 ½ x 19 ¾ x ⅛" (85 x 50 x 0.3 cm)

In 2003 the International Design Conference in Aspen, Colorado, supported an exhibition entitled *Head Guard* (see page 166). The exhibition covered a range of solutions to cultural and critical issues and offered different perceptions of basic emotions.

Designers, artists, and students at the Bezalel Academy of Art and Design in Jerusalem joined in developing a design for protective masks that could be used daily. It began with the premise that the first instinct in facing a dangerous situation was to protect one's head with one's arms. "Shielding the head is the first instinctive act. Revelation and veiling, protection and exposure of the head and the ways in which these actions are formed, are the litmus paper of humankind's cultural look," said Ezri Tarazi, head of the Department of Industrial Design at the Academy.

Reminiscent of the Muslim *hijab* and other head coverings, Galya Rosenfeld's Headscarf, made of stainless-steel knitted ball chain and secured with knitting needles, provides protection to a woman without annulling her identity. —P. J.

Neptunic C Sharksuit 2005

Jeremiah Sullivan (American, born 1954) and
Sang Sukcharoun (Cambodian, born 1960)
Stainless steel, nylon, and polycarbonate,
6' x 25" x 15" (183 x 63.5 x 38 cm)
Manufacturer: Neptunic Sharksuits, USA (2005)

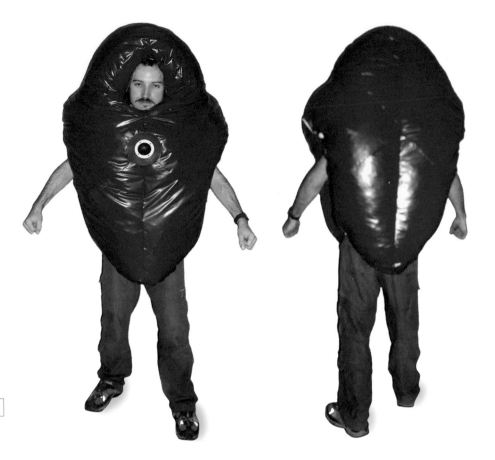

Suited for Subversion Prototype. 2002

Ralph Borland (South African, born 1974)
Nylon-reinforced PVC, padding, speaker, and pulse reader,
47 ¼ x 31 ½ x 23 ⅝" (120 x 80 x 60 cm)

Suited for Subversion is a civil-disobedience suit to be worn by street protesters to protect themselves from police batons. More than just a shield, the suit is a conceptual statement, drawing attention to the risks that a protester has to face in order to defend his convictions.

The idea of the suit draws on the "white overall" tactics of organizations like Wombles, Ya Basta!, or Tute Bianche. White Overalls is an anticapitalist movement that originated in Italy. Its members dress entirely in white overalls, padded with bubble wrap and polystyrene. Sometimes they wear gas masks to hide their identities. Their protective wear is a safeguard and a way to create spectacle, attract people's attention, and encourage society to echo their senti-

ments. Another source of inspiration for Ralph Borland was the Barcelonian design group Las Agencias, which exaggerates the theatricality of protest groups with humorous solutions like their colorful *prêt-à-revolter* line of clothing.

In Borland's design, a wireless video camera mounted over the head acts like a witness and records police action. The system transmits the signal directly to a control station, obviating the need for a tape that could be destroyed, thus losing evidence.

A speaker in the center of the chest amplifies and projects the wearer's heartbeat, or can also be used to play music or chant slogans. In a group action, when many people are wearing these suits, one would hear heartbeats increasing as tension and excitement mount, like a natural soundtrack arousing the crowd. At the same time, the heartbeat exposes the vulnerability of the individual. The fragility of the human body is exploited as a tool, a shield, almost as a weapon, against police munitions.   —P. J.

Bulletproof Quilted Duvet Prototype. 2004

Tobias Wong (Canadian, born 1974)
Ballistic nylon, cotton, and cotton flannel,
7' 2" x 7' 2" (218.5 x 218.5 cm)
Prototype by Tobias Wong, quilting by Peggy Konkol of
Harbor Lights Quilting, Canada (2004)

Ballistic Rose Brooch 2004

Tobias Wong (Canadian, born 1974)
Ballistic nylon, velvet leaves, and silver pin,
5" (13 cm) diam.
Manufacturer: Conduit Group, USA (2004)

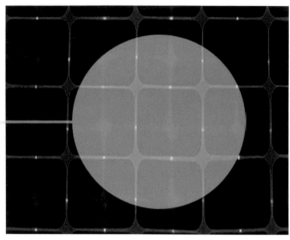

T-shirt and **vest** (above) Prototype. 2004
Polycarbonate and cotton, 28 ¾ x 21 ⅝" (73 x 55 cm)

Killing Zones shirt (right) Prototype. 2004
Metal foil and cotton, 31 ½ x 24 ¾" (80 x 63 cm)

Arik Levy (Israeli, born 1963), **Tal Lancman** (Israeli,
born 1962), and **Maurizio Galante** (Italian, born 1963)
Prototypes by Interware SARL and Ldesign SARL,
France (2005)

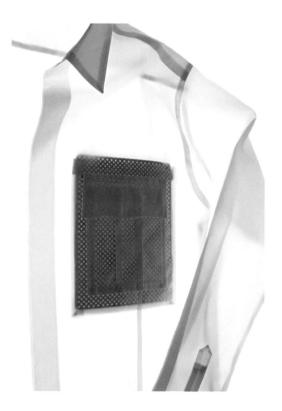

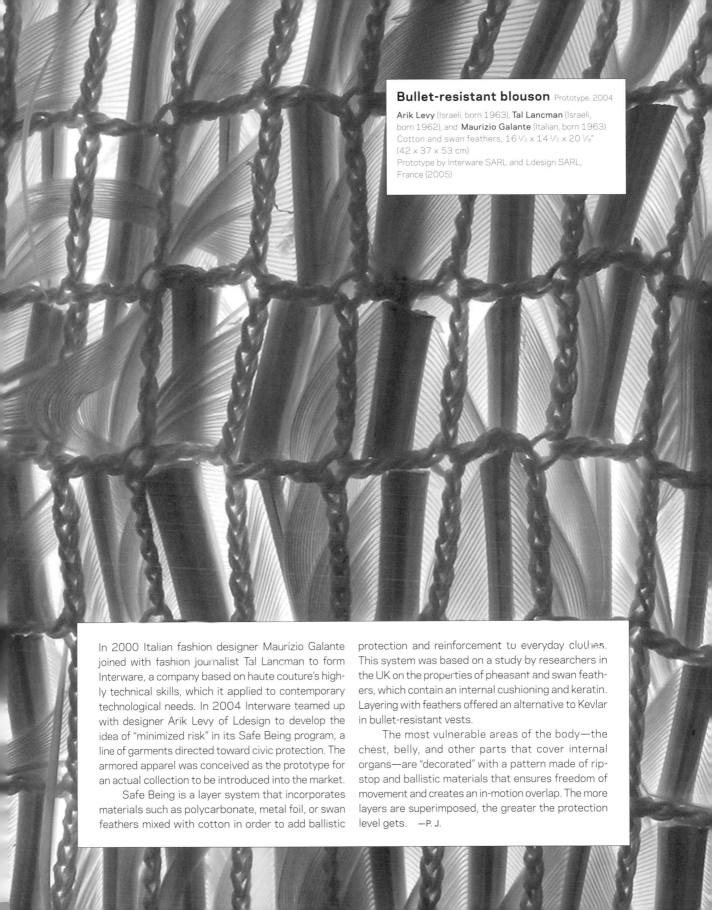

Bullet-resistant blouson Prototype. 2004

Arik Levy (Israeli, born 1963), Tal Lancman (Israeli, born 1962), and Maurizio Galante (Italian, born 1963)
Cotton and swan feathers, 16 1/2 x 14 1/2 x 20 7/8"
(42 x 37 x 53 cm)
Prototype by Interware SARL and Ldesign SARL, France (2005)

In 2000 Italian fashion designer Maurizio Galante joined with fashion journalist Tal Lancman to form Interware, a company based on haute couture's highly technical skills, which it applied to contemporary technological needs. In 2004 Interware teamed up with designer Arik Levy of Ldesign to develop the idea of "minimized risk" in its Safe Being program, a line of garments directed toward civic protection. The armored apparel was conceived as the prototype for an actual collection to be introduced into the market.

Safe Being is a layer system that incorporates materials such as polycarbonate, metal foil, or swan feathers mixed with cotton in order to add ballistic protection and reinforcement to everyday clothes. This system was based on a study by researchers in the UK on the properties of pheasant and swan feathers, which contain an internal cushioning and keratin. Layering with feathers offered an alternative to Kevlar in bullet-resistant vests.

The most vulnerable areas of the body—the chest, belly, and other parts that cover internal organs—are "decorated" with a pattern made of ripstop and ballistic materials that ensures freedom of movement and creates an in-motion overlap. The more layers are superimposed, the greater the protection level gets. —P. J.

CHP 100 Conical Hand Protector 2001

Med-Eng Systems, Inc. (Canada, est. 1981)
Thermoplastic polymers, Kevlar, and reinforced rubber,
7 ⅞ x 7 ⅛" (20 x 18 cm) diam.
Manufacturer: Med-Eng Systems, Inc., Canada (2002)

Oyster Glove chain mail glove 1995

Carl Mertens, company design (Germany, est. 1919)
Stainless steel
Manufacturer: Carl Mertens, Germany (1995)

Static Dissipative Finger Cots 1985

North Safety Products Development and
Manufacturing Team (USA, est. 1973)
Natural rubber, 2 ¾ x 1 ³⁄₁₆" (7 x 3 cm)
Manufacturer: North Safety Products, USA (1985)

Silver Shield/4H
Chemical-Resistant Booties 1987

North Safety Products Development and
Manufacturing Team (USA, est. 1973)
Polyethylene and EVA plastics, 16 x 14" (40.6 x 33.5 cm)
Manufacturer: North Safety Products, USA (1987)

Industrial Overshoe / TPU 12 2002

Scott Hardy (American, born 1968) and
Steve Opie (American, born 1960)
Urethane
Manufacturer: NEOS, New England Overshoe
Company, Inc., USA (2003)

Lumber pro class 3 Safety Boot 2002

Glenn Elkstrand (Swedish, born 1960)
Tretorn (Swedish, est. 1891)
Natural rubber, nitrile rubber, cotton, Pe/cotton 50/50,
and 3D textile
Manufacturer: Fagum-Stomil S.A., Poland (2003)

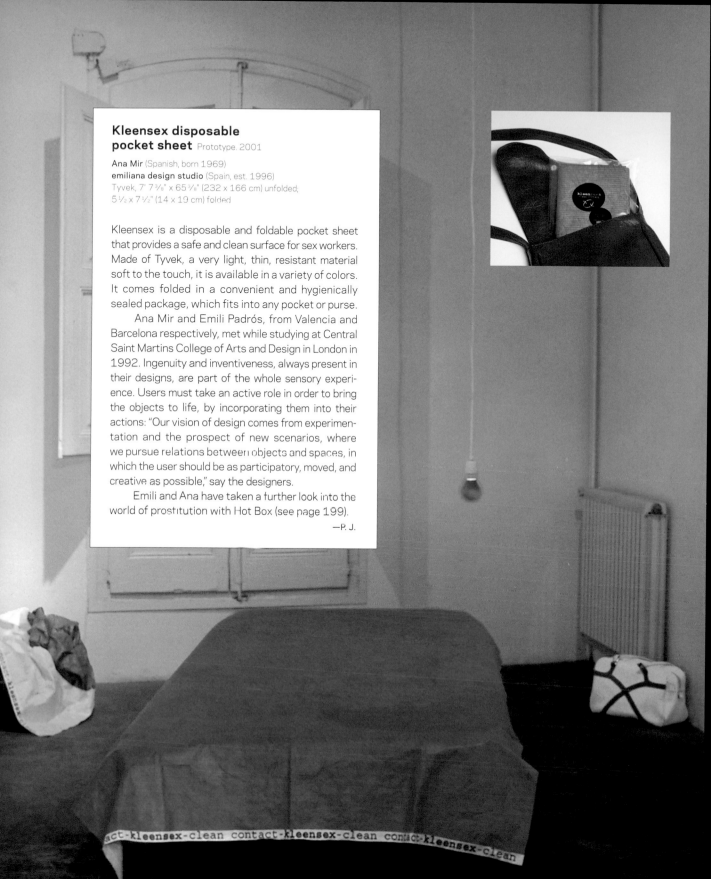

Kleensex disposable
pocket sheet Prototype. 2001

Ana Mir (Spanish, born 1969)
emiliana design studio (Spain, est. 1996)
Tyvek, 7' 7 ³⁄₈" x 65 ³⁄₈" (232 x 166 cm) unfolded;
5 ½ x 7 ½" (14 x 19 cm) folded

Kleensex is a disposable and foldable pocket sheet
that provides a safe and clean surface for sex workers.
Made of Tyvek, a very light, thin, resistant material
soft to the touch, it is available in a variety of colors.
It comes folded in a convenient and hygienically
sealed package, which fits into any pocket or purse.

Ana Mir and Emili Padrós, from Valencia and
Barcelona respectively, met while studying at Central
Saint Martins College of Arts and Design in London in
1992. Ingenuity and inventiveness, always present in
their designs, are part of the whole sensory experience. Users must take an active role in order to bring
the objects to life, by incorporating them into their
actions: "Our vision of design comes from experimen-
tation and the prospect of new scenarios, where
we pursue relations between objects and spaces, in
which the user should be as participatory, moved, and
creative as possible," say the designers.

Emili and Ana have taken a further look into the
world of prostitution with Hot Box (see page 199).

—P. J.

ABOBA Blood Type Condoms 1985

Osaka Senden Kenkyusho Co., Ltd. (Japan, est. 1965)
Latex, 3 ⅛ x 2 ½ x ¾" (8.1 x 6.1 x 2 cm)
Manufacturer: Jex, Inc., Japan (1985)

Condom Applicator 2004

Roelf Mulder (South African, born 1959), Byron Qually
(South African, born 1973), and Richard Perez (South
African, born 1970) of ...XYZ Dot Dot Dot Ex Why Zed
Design, Ltd. (South Africa, est. 2000)
Polyethylene and aluminum, ¼ x 2 ¼ x 2 ⅛"
(0.75 x 5.5 x 5.5 cm)
Manufacturer: ...XYZ Dot Dot Dot Ex Why Zed Design, Ltd.,
South Africa (2005)

Despite widespread campaigns to inform the general
public about the importance of condoms, their use in
South Africa is still alarmingly low. The most often-
quoted reasons for not using them are: their application interferes with the sexual act and they are
not easy to remove from the package in the dark.
Moreover, applying the condom by hand is unhygienic and unsafe, and there is always the risk of
contaminating it if it is unrolled from the wrong side.

...XYZ industrial design firm, based in Cape
Town, South Africa, took up the challenge of creating
an applicator that was cheap, fast, user-friendly, and
no bigger than the usual packaging. The aim was to
improve on an existing product, not to introduce a new
system into an already controversial environment.

The innovative packaging allows the condom to
be unwrapped and fitted in three seconds. The applicator is sealed into a foil pouch with the condom.
When bent, the foil splits open on the correct side,
and the applicator pops off and slides out the condom.
This product could promote the use of condoms and
help reduce sexually transmitted diseases, hopefully
alleviating the HIV/AIDS pandemic in sub-Saharan
Africa. —P. J.

Mojo Barrier 1998

John Mulder (Dutch, born 1955) and
Rob de Boer (Dutch, born 1943)
Aluminum, 47¼ x 39⅜ x 49¼" (120 x 100 x 125 cm)
Manufacturer: Metaal 2000 BV, The Netherlands (1998)

Until the 1980s, security barriers to control crowds at concerts needed a structure to which they could be attached. They were usually affixed to the stage, making it difficult for security personnel to reach people in an emergency. A freestanding barrier would be safer and more efficient, organizers thought.

The result was the Mojo Barrier, a foldable, modular barrier system produced by Mojo Concerts, the leading concert promoter in the Netherlands. The weight of the crowd prevents the barrier from sliding and tipping over, yet it collapses in the event of a stampede, making it easier for the audience to escape. It also includes a step at the back that security and first-aid personnel can stand on to visually check the crowd.

The original barrier dates back to 1988; the current aluminum barrier was designed in 1998. Besides the aluminum barriers used in front of the stage, others, of recycled plastic with a stainless-steel serving top, can be enlisted to create bars, cloakrooms, and other services needed for a concert. Barriers can be joined together by sliding them against each other and securing them with a bolt. The Mojo Barrier is a system that includes special sections for curves, reverse corners, platforms, cableruns, gates, and emergency exits, as well as carts for transportation and storage, which makes it suitable for tours. The freestanding crowd-control barrier has become the world standard for big concerts by renowned bands. —P. J.

Con Edison Cast Iron Covers,
Type Q-8-V1, for Electric Manholes 2004

Gin L. Eng (American, born 1950) and Marco Meza
(American, born 1947) of Con Edison (USA, est. 1823)
Cast iron, 2' 7 7/8" (81 cm) diam.
Manufacturer: DuCast, United Arab Emirates, Shanxi Yuansheng
Industrial Co., China, ECCLES, China, and Creswell Manufacturing,
India (2005)

Beneath that ubiquitous urban object, the manhole cover, lies a complex world of wires and pipes. In this underground environment, operational conditions such as the buildup of vapors can affect the function of the cover. To address this situation, engineers constantly seek safer ways to improve the perform- ance of the cover while preserving its simple shape and its ability to tolerate the wear-and-tear of urban life. In this case, Con Edison (Consolidated Edison Company of New York), the private utility that deliv- ers electricity, gas, and steam service to the New York metropolitan area, set out to redesign a cover that would allow for ventilation, keep electrical cables and gas and steam pipelines hidden, with- stand heavy traffic vibrations, minimize water entry, and prevent excess accumulation of street debris. Weighing nearly three hundred pounds, the new manhole cover allows for twenty-six percent of the surface area to be open for ventilation.

Safety has played a powerful role in shaping civilized society. Were we to attempt an analysis of the history of mankind, we would have to tackle the subject of how property and ownership have been safeguarded or exploited. Wars and revolutions have been justified by the need to take, defend, or negate possession of countries and social systems.

At a scale more attainable by design, fear of theft and destruction of property have stimulated the invention of many archetypical devices. Urban planners and architects have always incorporated visible protective barriers into their designs, from moats and city walls to locks and fences. Several contemporary solutions to protect buildings have gone the way of much design and become invisible to the average person. Yet even the most sophisticated alarm system, which can perhaps prevent break-ins and burglaries, cannot do much to stop terrorists. To this point, some architects have rediscovered the typology of the moat and devised new protective belts around buildings that are more akin to hidden bear traps than to

property

walls. In the latter instance, the weight of an approaching car bomb would break the sidewalk and let it fall into the trap at a safe distance from the building.

When personal defense and the defense of one's property against a direct offensive attack are at issue, designers have sometimes tried to mask protection under a decorative veil. Beautiful, complex facades that are meant to deflect and dissipate the impact of a bomb on a building; iron fences topped by cute bunny rabbits; elegant bar chairs modified to accommodate hooks for purses, to protect against their theft; delicate rings that become brass knuckles for self-defense; bedside tables that can be turned into baseball bats and shields—if we have to live in anxiety, designers suggest we turn objects that we need because of our anxiety into something beautiful, sublime, uplifting, delightful.

While the need to protect ourselves and our personal possessions is as old as civilization itself, the idea of identity theft is more recent. Kings and popes once marked their identities with seal rings, while ordinary people presented paper passe-partouts, identity cards, or passports. These paper IDs were once relatively hard to counterfeit. Today, identity theft has become rampant, as we entrust our identity to a few unreliable passwords and to the good will of the innumerable institutions that manipulate our data. As a consequence, the need to reaffirm one's identity and beliefs—whether by wearing a name necklace, acquiring a tattoo, or signing a living will—and to make sure one's personality cannot be sidelined or overstepped offer major opportunities for design to have influence.

One recent development brought about by the dematerialization of money into magnetically recordable debt, and by the connection of the whole world of transactions into a seamless network, is the protection of digital identity. Authenticity, the key to the effective protection of one's identity, is design's eternal endeavor. —P. A.

NoGo Barrier New York Financial District Streetscape and Security Design 2004

Robert Rogers (American, born 1959), Jonathan Marvel (American, born 1960), Richard Ramsey (American, born 1967), Tim Fryatt (American, born 1973), and Graeme Waitzkin (American, born 1979) of Rogers Marvel Architects, PLLC (USA, est. 1992)
Bronze, concrete, and steel, 33 x 52 x 45"
(84 x 132 x 114 cm)
Manufacturer: Kevin Biebel, J. Frederick Construction, Inc., USA (2004)

Monolith, **Tripart**, and **Oobelisk**, **Security Bollards** Prototypes, 2004

Frederick Arlen Reeder (American, born 1948)
Stainless steel, Monolith: 40 x 11" (101.5 x 28 cm) base diam.; Tripart: 36 x 9 ½" (91.5 x 24 cm) triangular base; Oobelisk: 40 x 8 ½" (101.5 x 21.5 cm) square base
Prototype by SO WORKS Site Objects for Perimeter Force Protection, USA (2004)

Barrier Bench Prototype. 2002

Philippe Million (French, born 1967)
Galvanized steel, 37 ⅜" x 6' ½" x 23 ⅝"
(95 x 184 x 60 cm)

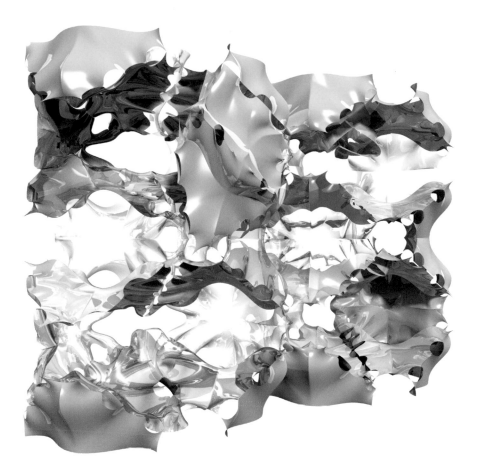

INVERSAbrane invertible
building membrane Prototype. 2005

Sulan Kolatan (American, born Turkey 1958) and
Bill McDonald (American, born 1956) of
Kolatan/Mac Donald Studio (USA, est. 1988)
Vacuum-formed DuPont Corian and Sentry impact-resistant glass
Prototype by Evans & Paul, Unlimited Corporation, USA (2005)

Like a skin, the facade of a building is the point of
contact with its surroundings as well as its ultimate
protection against it. Architects KOL/MAC have
developed a method of coexistence for city and
structure by maximizing the physical contact
between a building and the air and space around it.
The INVERSAbrane is an invertible building membrane designed with excess surface area that acts
as a defensive, yet proactive barrier between the
elements and the structure it defends. The mem
brane circulates air, filtering out pollutants and other
allergens. Its bladders collect rainwater for daily use
as well as for sprinkler action; the surfaces use solar
energy to regulate humidity and temperature both
inside and out. Wind velocities are minimized
through deceleration. INVERSAbrane incorporates
materials with a performance-rating high in safety
and comfort, such as fire-resistant and thermoactive
textiles, and includes biomedia as a biofiltration
mechanism, thereby becoming a nutritional and
physical substrate to microorganisms. It can be integrated into other systems and is suitable for both
new and existing buildings.   —R. L.

Sweet Dreams Security series of safety products, shown on pages 100–102, is Matthias Megyeri's comment on the growing demand for security in our modern culture, mixed with the saturation of exaggerated niceness in everything that surrounds us: iron railings with bunny rabbits for posts; barbed wire with angular butterflies and fish; personalized, sharp glass shards to top a brick wall; heart-shaped ring chains with teddy-bear padlocks; catlike CCTV cameras with bat wings; and burglar-alarm boxes crowned by daisies.

Megyeri's work as a student at the Royal College of Art in London largely focused on security in a domestic environment, taking a critical and ironic look at the contradictory attitudes toward it. Responding to an assignment to design a placebo product for a psychological illness or phobia, Sweet Dreams Security focused on the heightened fears associated with home security. The resulting products merged the need for protection with the desire for beauty, redefining padlocks, fences, and razor wire as loveable objects.

Megyeri's photographs of London, which juxtapose the need for protection and the desire for beauty in the urban landscape, were the inspiration for this project. His security products are designed for the space between the home and the street, drawing boundaries between private and public. The project is still evolving, with new designs underway, and is moving toward products for personal safety inside the house and at the office. There is an endless variety of arrangements, depending on the concerns addressed. The new objects will emphasize Megyeri's overriding message: "It's still form follows function. It's just that the function is more psychological than ergonomic." —P. J.

Peter Pin, **R. Bunnit**, and **Didoo Railings** 2003

Matthias Megyeri (German, born 1973)
Iron, 70 7/8" (180 cm) high
Manufacturer: Marbek, UK, and Matthias Megyeri, Germany (2005)

Mr. Smish & Madame Buttly
Razor Wire Prototype. 2003

Matthias Megyeri (German, born 1973)
Steel, 15 ¾ x 15 ¾" (40 x 40 cm) x desired length

Landscape
Glass Objects series Prototype. 2003

Matthias Megyeri (German, born 1973)
Recycled glass, each 4 ¾ x 2 x 1 ⅛" (12 x 5 x 3 cm)

Heart to Heart chain from the
Sweet Dreams Security series Prototype. 2004

Matthias Megyeri (German, born 1973)
Iron, each link 2 ½ x 2" (7 x 5 cm)

Billy B. Old English Padlock from the
Sweet Dreams Security series Prototype. 2003

Matthias Megyeri (German, born 1973)
Steel and brass, ⅞ x 2 ¾ x ¾" (10 x 7 x 2 cm)

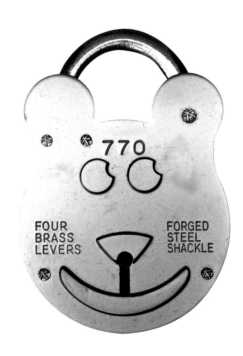

Puma Bike from the **Puma Tribranded Collection** 2004

Jens Martin Skibsted (Danish, born 1970), **Biomega** (Denmark, est. 1998), and **Adam Thorpe** (Welsh, born 1969) and **Joe Hunter** (British, born 1967) of **Vexed Generation** (UK, est. 1994)
Aluminum, 59 x 42 ⅛" (150 x 107 cm) unfolded;
37 ¾ x 22" (96 x 56 cm) folded
Manufacturer: Puma, Germany (2005)

Jens Martin Skibsted conceived the company Biomega while visiting Antoni Gaudí's buildings in Barcelona. Touched and inspired by Gaudí's visionary synthesis of technology and invention, he vowed to move his designs in the same direction, with the aim of making cities better places and the bike the means to this end. Biomega reacts to our sedentary society and polluted environment by setting new and unique standards for commuting around towns and cities. The countermovement Urban Mobility is its technologic, moral, and aesthetic response to a hostile urban setting: "Urban Mobility is about commuting effectively and in style within the city environment," Skibsted explains.

Biomega, Vexed Generation (see page 108), and the sports-equipment manufacturer Puma joined forces to launch a limited edition called Tribranded Collection as part of the Urban Mobility line. It consists of a bike and a range of accessories and garments designed for ease of movement and everyday commuting. The Puma Bike created by Skibsted is the result of this collaborative initiative.

Skibsted's design recognizes the new challenges that the equipment faces and the constant need for "bipolar functionalities"—riding and walking, accelerating and braking. The Puma Bike has a folding mechanism that differs from a regular folding bike in that it allows the bike to be reduced in size by fifty percent to fit in tight spaces like an elevator, a bus or subway, or a small apartment. Its main feature is a locking mechanism integrated within the structural framework of the bike, so that if someone tries to steal it and breaks the lock, the bicycle breaks as well. At the same time, this system obviates the need for a separate lock, maximizing the bike's ease of use.

Biomega is also part of an ongoing project on bike safety conducted by Design against Crime (see page 104). Bicycle users can post their photographs and comments on bike commuting and parking in the forumlike Web site www.bikeoff.org. —P. J.

Stop Thief! Ply Chair Prototype. 2000

Jackie Piper (American, born UK 1968),
Marcus Willcocks (British, born 1977), and
Lorraine Gamman (British, born 1957)
Design against Crime Research Initiative, Central
Saint Martins College of Art and Design (UK, est. 2000)
Laminated plywood, 3 ⅜ x 17 ⅛ x 19 ¼"
(8.45 x 43.5 x 49 cm)

Design against Crime is an initiative that originated at the University of the Arts London in 2000, under the auspices of Central Saint Martins College of Art and Design and the London Institute. Its aim is to give an appealing edge to anticrime design. The philosophy behind the program is that security and safety designs do not have to look hostile. Designers need to be far more creative and adaptable than delinquents, designing products, services, graphic material, and environments that address the user, not just the abuser.

Each project in this initiative to help prevent and reduce crime begins by studying the existing problems and analyzing potential theft situations. A crime-prevention study, undertaken with criminologists and experts from the Jill Dando Institute of Crime Science in London and other organizations, is followed by field research conducted by Central Saint Martins. This preliminary inquiry helps to identify the relevant questions to be addressed and establish the criteria to evaluate the proposals.

Under the direction of Lorraine Gamman, Design against Crime has undertaken several research and design projects, seminars, workshops, and exhibitions on crime-related issues.

The Stop Thief! Smart Antitheft Furniture focuses on the customizing of some five iconic chairs, adding specific features to make them more secure against theft. The Stop Thief! Ply Chair and Stop Thief! Bentwood Chair Clone are the improved versions of the Arne Jacobsen's Series 7 chair and of a Thonet chair, respectively. The intention is to extend the particular features of these chairs with a visually integrated solution that fits their shape and materials.

This antitheft furniture was designed to improve the safety and comfort of customers in a restaurant or café by allowing them to secure their belongings to the seat. At the same time it was meant not to disturb the overall atmosphere of the surroundings. The prototypes were tested in-situ at restaurants in Covent Garden and other sites in Central London.   —P. J.

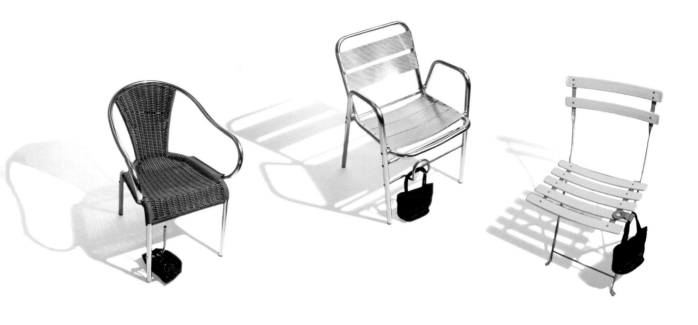

Stop Thief! Bentwood Chair Clone
Prototype. 2000

Jackie Piper (American, born UK 1968),
Marcus Willcocks (British, born 1977), and
Lorraine Gamman (British, born 1957)
Design against Crime Research Initiative, Central
Saint Martins College of Art and Design (UK, est. 2000)
Wood, 34 ½ x 16 ⅛ x 20 ⅞" (87.5 x 41 x 53 cm)

"Keep Your Bag Safe!" Flyer 2004

Sean O'Mara (Irish, born The Netherlands 1967), **Chris Thomas**
(British, born 1978), **Marcus Willcocks** (British, born 1977), and
Lorraine Gamman (British, born 1957)
**Design against Crime Research Initiative, Central
Saint Martins College of Art and Design** (UK, est. 2000)
Laminated paper, 5⅜ x 4⅛" (13.5 x 10.5 cm)
Manufacturers: Design against Crime Research Initiative
and Kingsland Color, UK (2004)

The flyer was part of a campaign to reduce bag
theft in London during the 2004 Christmas season.
Working with the Metropolitan Police and the London
and Westminster Council, Design against Crime
created a communication strategy to alert shoppers
to the proliferation of bag thieves in the Soho area.

A package of graphic material was issued by
crime-prevention officers to bars, cafés, and food
stores in the borough of Westminster: tabletop leaflets
in eight languages informed of the types of theft that
could occur and the objects that were most commonly targeted; posters were placed in toilets and public
areas; and handbag-like flyers that delivered warning messages were placed over the necks of wine or
beer bottles.   —P. J.

PowerPizza 2001

Chris Vanstone (Welsh, born 1977) and **Mickaël
Charbonnel** (French, born 1977) of **Human Beans**
(UK, est. 2001)
Italian style pizza box, foam, and Velcro,
15 x 15 x 1⅞" (38 x 38 x 4.7 cm)
Manufacturer: Marion Gillet, Creative Product
Development, UK (2004)

Sporran-Utan Prototype. 2000

Paul Yuille (Scottish, born 1976)
Design against Crime Research Initiative, Central
Saint Martins College of Art and Design (UK, est. 2000)
Sheepskin, 4⅜ x 11¾ x 16½" (11 x 30 x 42 cm)

Zone OneandTwo Prototype. 2000

Hedi Raikamo (Finnish, born 1965)
Design against Crime Research Initiative, Central Saint
Martins College of Art and Design (UK, est. 2000)
Calfskin, 1⅝ x 12¾ x 16½" (4 x 32.5 x 42 cm)

The In the Bag project was developed by the students at Central Saint Martins College of Art and Design in collaboration with the Metropolitan Police, British Transport Police, and the Home Office. The proposals responded to four main types of bag theft, addressing one or more of the following possibilities: dipping—the removal of articles from a bag without the owner's awareness; slashing—the removal of articles by cutting the fabric; lifting—the removal of the bag without the owner's knowledge; and grabbing—the removal of a bag by snatching it away from the owner's grasp. The project was therefore concerned about use, misuse, and abuse: potential theft.

The Sporran-Utan furry bag gets its name and features from the traditional Scottish sporran, the front purse that complements the kilt. Like the sporran, it is worn over the groin area, giving the user complete control over the bag. The long sheepskin makes it difficult for the thief to find access to the inside, and the manner in which it is worn makes it difficult to attempt robbery without being noticed.

Zone OneandTwo is a leather handbag also worn at the front of the body, with open pockets that work like a muff and zippered pockets that block access to intruders but are easily reachable by the wearer. —P. J.

Scroll Top Backpack (above) 2001

Cordura, wire, foam, nylon, and Velcro, 22 x 11¾ x 5⅛"
(56 x 30 x 13 cm) open; 15½ x 11¾ x 5⅛"
(39.5 x 30 x 13 cm) closed

Karryfront Screamer bag (left) 2001

Cordura, wire, padding, nylon, and antiattack alarm,
15 x 10⅝ x 2¾" (38 x 27 x 7 cm)

Adam Thorpe (Welsh, born 1969) and **Joe Hunter**
(British, born 1967) of **Vexed Generation** (UK, est. 1994)
**Design against Crime Research Initiative, Central
Saint Martins College of Art and Design** (UK, est. 2000)
Manufacturer: Karrysafe, UK (2001)

In 2002 Design against Crime collaborated with clothing designers Adam Thorpe and Joe Hunter of Vexed Generation to develop the Karrysafe line of antitheft bags and wearable accessories. Established in London in 1994, Vexed Generation produces clothes that suit an urban setting and promote environmental and social issues. Air pollution, surveillance, and civil liberties are often addressed by incorporating unique design solutions and technologies, like respiratory protection or high-performance fabrics that are waterproof, breathable, reflective, fire-retardant, and knife-resistant (see page 198). Some pieces are specifically designed for bike users, since the designers of Vexed Generation consider biking the ideal means of transportation in an urban setting (see page 103).

The philosophy of this design initiative is that the best protection against crime is awareness and the willingness to take some basic precautions in public places. The bags incorporate materials and electronic technologies used in the automotive and aircraft industries, such as Cordura—a high-performance durable textile material resistant to abrasion—and electronic alarms. Both systems can be found in the Karryfront Screamer laptop bag. The built-in antiattack alarm will automatically start "screaming" at 138 decibels if the bag is forcibly removed from its owner. The two-way strap allows the option of carrying it across the front while walking or on the back if cycling. Another variant, the Scroll Top Backpack, features a Velcro scrolling top that avoids dipping, as its noise will alert the owner. It is made of slash-proof materials and has an antilifting clip and a double-thick strap that make access even more difficult.

The Phonesafe wrist holder (opposite) offers a hand-free way of carrying a cell phone and is slim enough to be worn under clothes, with additional pockets for cards and keys. It also lets the user receive calls without removing the phone from the stretch pouch.

With design focused on users' needs, these accessories are meant to resist any attempt of aggression and discourage street robbers and pickpockets. —P. J.

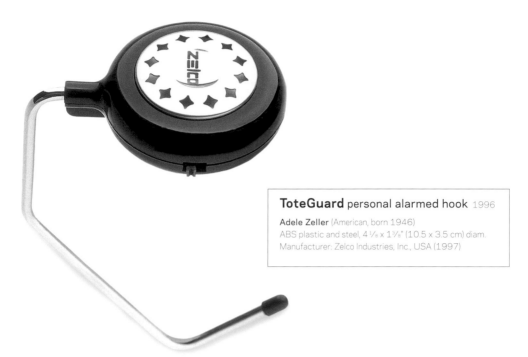

ToteGuard personal alarmed hook 1996

Adele Zeller (American, born 1946)
ABS plastic and steel, 4 ⅛ x 1 ⅜" (10.5 x 3.5 cm) diam.
Manufacturer: Zelco Industries, Inc., USA (1997)

Phonesafe 2001

Adam Thorpe (Welsh, born 1969) and Joe Hunter
(British, born 1967) of **Vexed Generation** (UK, est. 1994)
**Design against Crime Research Initiative, Central
Saint Martins College of Art and Design** (UK, est. 2000)
PowerNet nylon and Spandex, ½ x ⅛" (1.4 x 0.2 cm)
Manufacturer: Karrysafe, UK (2001)

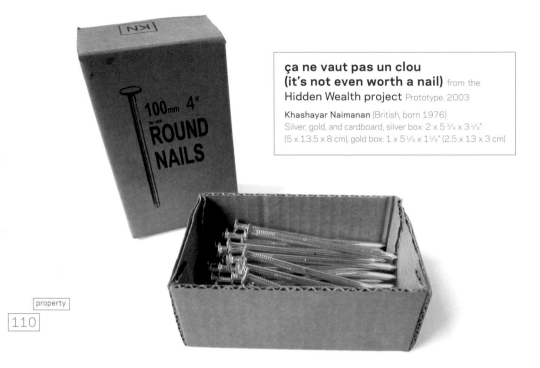

**ça ne vaut pas un clou
(it's not even worth a nail)** from the
Hidden Wealth project Prototype. 2003

Khashayar Naimanan (British, born 1976)
Silver, gold, and cardboard, silver box: 2 x 5 ⅜ x 3 ⅛"
(5 x 13.5 x 8 cm); gold box: 1 x 5 ⅛ x 1 ⅛" (2.5 x 13 x 3 cm)

British designer Khashayar Naimanan suggests an alternative to traditional ways of hiding valuable belongings by concealing them within objects that are not usually associated with wealth. In *ça ne vaut pas un clou*, gold and silver were shaped into four-inch nails reminiscent of normal humble nails. These precious metals are thus hidden within a common shape that is not perceived as valuable. This design also alludes to standard places for hiding wealth, such as safes behind paintings.

Incognito is a set of tableware produced by Porzellan-Manufaktur Nymphenburg in Germany (opposite). The classic Rococo hand-painted detailing distinguishes it as a luxury item. However, the precious motifs have been deliberately hidden and are only revealed when a piece is turned upside down. The modest appearance of the china contrasts with the precious detailing underneath, suggesting a history and tradition, and a value, that are not revealed by its ordinary appearance. —P. J.

Incognito dinnerware from the
Hidden Wealth project 2003

Khashayar Naimanan (British, born 1976)
Porcelain, dimensions variable
Manufacturer: Porzellan-Manufaktur Nymphenburg,
Germany (2005)

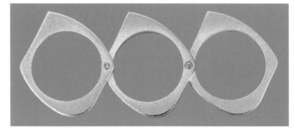

Subtle Safety Defensive Ring 2003

Amanda Knox (American, born 1975), **Kim Hoffmann** (American, born 1975), and **Sara Shaughnessy** (American, born 1979) of **RedStart Design, LLC** (USA, est. 2004)
Sterling silver and stainless steel, 1 x 1 x ½" (2.5 x 2.5 x 1 cm)
Manufacturer: RedStart Design, LLC, USA (2004)

RedStart Design, a jewelry design company, is the result of a collaboration between engineers and artists, and the Subtle Safety Defensive Ring is the product of that union. This accessory is meant to be used primarily as a method of empowerment for women, not to take the place of self-defense classes but to provide a measure of safety to a woman walking alone at night. The ring is an alternative solution to the recommended practice of a woman placing her keys between her fingers in case of attack. The ring is more stable, slipping over three fingers; it requires less coordination to be effective; and it allows the wearer to free up her keys for easier and quicker access to her car or home. When not used for defense, the ring folds in on itself, taking the form of an elegant stack of three shapes, and can be worn on one finger as a decorative accessory. —R. L.

Guardian Angel handbag 2002

Carolien Vlieger (Dutch, born 1975) and
Hein van Dam (Dutch, born 1974)
Leather and wool felt, 13 x 10 x 3" (33 x 26 x 8 cm)
Manufacturer: Vlieger & Vandam, The Netherlands (2004)

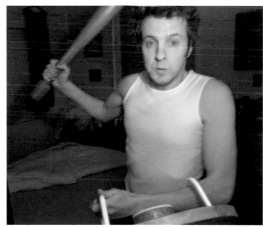

Safe Bedside Table Prototype. 2002

James McAdam (British, born 1977)
Cherry wood and steel, 23 ⅝ x 17 ¾" (60 x 45 cm) diam.

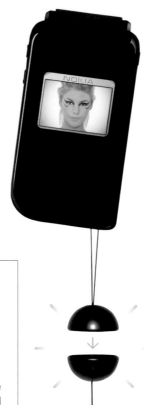

Ballistic Assault Alarm
Cell-Phone Charm 2004

Mattias Ståhlbom (Swedish, born 1971)
TAF Arkitektkontor AB (Sweden, est. 2002)
Rubber, 4 x 1⅛" (10 x 3 cm) diam.
Manufacturer: Blingks, Sweden (2005)

The proliferation of mobile phones has triggered the appearance of all kinds of accessories associated with their use. Some of them are merely decorative, while others also have a functional purpose.

Two cell-phone charms designed by Mattias Ståhlbom were commissioned by Blingks, the Swedish maker of mobile accessories, as part of a product line called Statements. The Ballistic Assault Alarm Charm has a strident siren that goes off when the rubber sphere is pulled, so that during an attempted theft or other aggressive act, this decorative and harmless object becomes an effective safety aid. A second charm, Libido, included in the exhibition, is a condom protection box made of hard plastic or aluminum that keeps the sensitive prophylactic intact and always within reach. It also works as a signal to other available singles.   —P. J.

Hair Card Concept. 2000

Pontus Wahlgren (Swedish, born 1974)
IDEO (USA, est. 1978)
Paper, 2 x 3½" (5 x 9 cm)

Courtesy Blood Card Concept. 2000

Monina Johnson Dolan (American, born 1971)
IDEO (USA, est. 1978)
Paper, 2 x 3½" (5 x 9 cm)

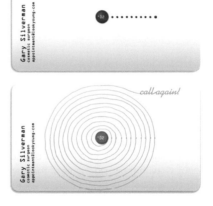

Seed Card Concept. 2000

Rico Zorkendorfer (German, born 1972)
IDEO (USA, est. 1978)
Paper, 2 x 3½" (5 x 9 cm)

As Time Goes By card Concept. 2000

Marion Buchenau (German, born 1968)
IDEO (USA, est. 1978)
Paper, 2 x 3½" (5 x 9 cm)

Recognizing that there are issues of identity and community in a business setting and a marked difficulty in protecting one's identity on the Internet, the IDEO team, in its conceptual series Identity Card Exploration, has focused on these issues, creating twenty cards to date.

The Hair Card and the Blood Card both contain the very essence of an individual's DNA, thus indicating to the recipients of these cards that the presenter has nothing to hide. These cards also draw attention to the ever-growing practice of companies asking their employees to submit to blood tests.

Some of the cards contain methods of jogging the memory that help link the card to its owner or virtually illustrate the growing and evolving relationship between people after their first meeting. A small plant sprouts from the Seed Card, which matures as the exchange between the recipient of the card and its presenter increases. The As Time Goes By card combats the monotony of exchanging business cards by transforming itself over time: the spiral shape grows larger to show the "life span" of the card, playing on the idea of counting the rings on a tree stump to determine its age. —R. L.

Bloomberg bUNIT
Personal Authentication Device 2004

Masamichi Udagawa (Japanese, born 1964) and
Sigi Moeslinger (Austrian, born 1968) of **Antenna Design**
(USA, est. 1997)
Helmars Ozolins (American, born 1957) of **Bloomberg L.P.**
(USA, est. 1981)
Aluminum and ABS plastic, 3 ½ x 2 ⅛ x ⅛"
(8.85 x 5.4 x 0.4 cm)
Manufacturer: Bloomberg L.P., USA (2004)

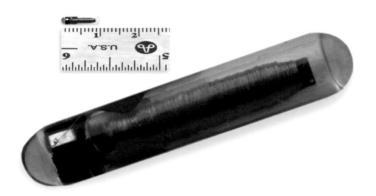

Trovan ID-100A Transponder
transdermal identification system 1999

Trovan Engineering Team (UK, est. 1988)
Biomedical glass, copper wire, and electronic components,
½ x ⅛" (1.15 x 0.21 cm) diam.
Manufacturer: Trovan, Ltd., UK (2005)

Do Not Resuscitate Necklace 1992

**Nederlandse Vereniging voor een Vrijwillig Levenseinde
(Right to Die-NL)** (The Netherlands, est. 1973)
Silver, 1 ⅛" (3 cm) diam.
Manufacturer: Koninklijke Begeer BV, The Netherlands (1992)

Refusing treatment for a critical injury or a terminal illness has been a legal right in the Netherlands since 1995. The WGBO law (the Act of Medical Treatment Agreement), which states that consent is necessary for all radical treatments, is not always observed by medical personnel. Living wills play a decisive role in this process, although they do not guarantee its outcome, since there is no such thing as "a right to euthanasia." Given the strict definition of euthanasia in the Dutch penal code, a doctor's decision not to use extraordinary measures to keep a person alive must be supported by an explicit request in the patient's will. In 2002 the Dutch Upper House approved the new euthanasia law: "exemption from criminal liability for the physician who, with due observance of the requirements of due care to be laid down by law, terminates a life on request or assists in a suicide of another person."

Members of the Nederlandse Vereniging voor een Vrijwillige Levenseinde (Right to Die-NL) are required to carry a Do Not Resuscitate document, which is similar in format to a credit card. The document expresses the wishes of its owner, asking the doctor not to extend life if there is no expectation of returning to a dignified state of living.

In addition to the card, the person can wear a special necklace that reads: *Niet Reanimeren* ("Do Not Resuscitate" in Dutch). As this necklace cannot bear a signature, it is not a legal document, but its significance lies in the fact that it will point the authorities to the official document, which is the will. Most importantly, it asserts a strong conviction: that under all circumstances the owner forbids any form of resuscitation. —P. J.

Every day, everywhere in the world, there is danger and anxiety. The causes for unease are dramatically different depending on political, socioeconomic, and geographic conditions. This chapter focuses on the exemplary and creative responses of designers all over the world to alleviate these concerns while taking into consideration the varied sets of circumstances they encounter.

In the United States, the accoutrements of safety range from door chains to seat belts, from advisory stickers on baby strollers to overstuffed boxes with polystyrene padding that protect electric appliances. In Japan, land of exemplary behavior, people who suffer from a cold wear surgical masks, while self-conscious business people can measure the quality of their breath before a meeting with the help of an electronic breath-checker available in any drugstore; they can also discharge their static electricity by means of a specially equipped keyholder before shaking hands. In India and Bangladesh, disposable covers are placed on pay phones to contain infectious diseases, and terra-cotta jars are used to filter arsenic out of water. In Cuba, bicycle bells are made of reused squeaky toys, raincoats are devised from sugar sacks, and home fences are made from discarded refrigerator grilles. Designers

everyday

are addressing the perception versus the reality of danger and making the best of the resources at hand, without losing sight of local culture and customs.

This chapter reads like a catalogue of fears that we encounter in routine, normal situations: fear of shattering our bones in a car accident or of an object breaking in the shipping process; fear of unsanitary conditions, diseases, bad smells, and hot handles; fear of ageing; fear of what smoking and overeating will do to us; fear of wasting water. We open it by breaking our rules about presenting objects of recent design, and show instead two eloquent logos from international shipping companies. Both logos express concisely and effectively our hopes for care and thoughtfulness in our daily life. Objects designed to make the world safer for children—and the elderly—have been produced in abundance in recent years, and there are now so many examples of exemplary design in this area that it was necessary to restrict ourselves to showing only a few.

Every chapter in this book has a culminating moment of irony, an exhortation to embrace our fears, and, in this instance, it is represented by a series of endearing stuffed toys portraying some of the most feared viruses and bacteria in the world (page 147). There is no end to this collection of fascinating anxieties. Especially in everyday life, safety is an industry in constant expansion, because, since there is no end to what could go wrong, there is also no end to the creative and commercial possibilities that design can offer.

—P. A.

**Kuroneko (black cat) logo for
Yamato Transport Co., Ltd.** 1957

Takeshi Shimizu (Japanese, n.d.)
Yamato Transport Co., Ltd. (Japan, est. 1919)

**Logo for Möbel-Transport
shipping company** (detail) c. 1964

Unknown designer (Swiss)
Möbel-Transport AG (Switzerland, est. 1961)

Nido Prototype. 2004

Pininfarina company design (Italy, est. 1930)
ABS, PMMA, and RTM plastics, Strandfoam polypropylene, aluminum, stainless steel, and cellular Inox 304 metal, 60⅜" x 66" x 9' 5¾" (153.4 x 167.4 x 289 cm)

Pininfarina's Nido concept has reexamined safety in small automobiles, redefining the current methodology of car production. The project involved an intense collaboration between designers and engineers, with the joint goal of creating a small, safe, and well-designed vehicle. Both aesthetic and technical concerns resulted in some innovative solutions.

The current trend of larger, heavier cars, which can cause major problems if they collide with smaller vehicles, heightened the need to address the issue of safety in a small, light car. Rather than basing the safety features of the car on its mass, Nido proposes a combination of three features: a chassis that supports the mechanical components, with a deformable front section and a rigid safety cell surrounding the occupants; a shell that holds the driver and passenger, which works like a sled that runs horizontally along a central rail; and two energy-dissipating absorbers that are made of honeycomb sections, connecting the chassis and the sled.

The novelty of the Nido car is its internal "crumple zone"—the predictable deformation spot that dissipates the impact of a crash before it is transmitted to the occupants. In the event of a frontal collision, the sled shifts forward and compresses the honeycomb absorbers, with a gradual and controlled deceleration of the passenger's compartment. Crash simulations proved the efficacy of the mobile sled system. The overall principle is also evident in the consistency of shape and structure; the single-box design gives a wider range of motion to the sled shell and conveys the sense of a protective nest (*nido* in Italian). —P. J.

takata04-neo child car seat 2004

Ichiro Iwasaki (Japanese, born 1965)
Polypropylene and polyester,
27 x 19¼ x 23" (68.5 x 48.9 x 58.5 cm)
Manufacturer: Takata Corporation, Japan (2004)

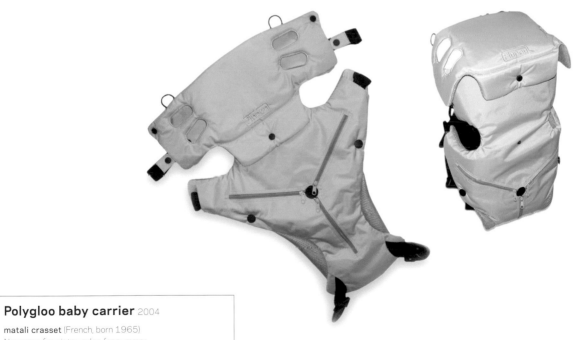

Polygloo baby carrier 2004

matali crasset (French, born 1965)
Neoprene for winter, nylon for summer,
17¾ x 21⅝" (45 x 55 cm)
Manufacturer: Pinpon, France (2005)

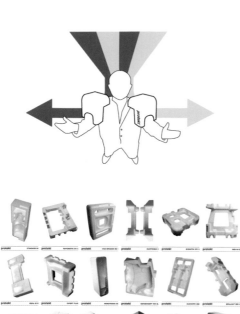

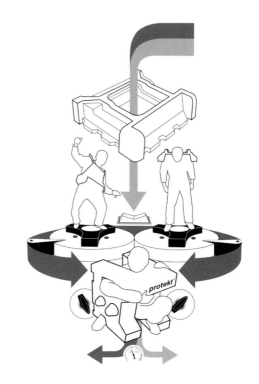

protekt, universal
protection set 2002-03

Paul Kirps (Luxembourgish, born 1969)
Offset/silk-screen print, 8½ x 11⅞" (21.5 x 30 cm) closed;
17 x 11⅞" (43 x 30 cm) open

Protekt is an imaginary brand, a visual game, the accidental result of the fusion of a pharmaceutical prescription and a household appliance, combined with the need to feel protected as part of human nature.

The project started with polystyrene packaging, such as that used in shipping electrical appliances. Normally, after an appliance has been unpacked, the packaging become useless and is thrown away. But the packaging forms themselves are uniquely created to protect the product and are often complex in shape, although none are conceived with an aesthetic consideration in mind. Graphic designer Paul Kirps borrowed those shapes and removed them from their familiar context to sketch a new visual language, presenting them as a functional product under the fictitious brand name "protekt."

The visual set has been collected in a product portfolio that consists of nine postcards, six A5-size cards—with all the different models—two A3-size posters, a sticker, and a leaflet with instructions; a "treatment" halfway between information design and pharmaceutical identity or between assembly instructions and prescription dosage. These fictional objects with imaginary functions, with names such as Turbomatik 1600, Duotronic 440, or Konsecuent 64, represent a solution for anxiety, a primary armor against all kinds of aggression, and a response to our daily fears and worries. In this utopian kit of universal protection, only the product is missing, yet it is still as present and as psychologically effective as the real thing. —P. J.

protekt©
universal protection set

SURROUND 9000	TURBOMATIK 160	STANDARD SV 90
RAPIDMATIK 24 C	VARIABEL 100 SB	DYNAMIK-PRO 80
EXPERT PLUS 90	PRO-MASTER 80	VARIABEL 550 XL

protekt©
universal protection set

SURROUND 9000	TURBOMATIK 160	STANDARD SV 90
RAPIDMATIK 24 C	VARIABEL 100 SB	DYNAMIK-PRO 80
EXPERT PLUS 90	PRO-MASTER 80	VARIABEL 550 XL

protekt©
universal protection set

MODULAR 5533 I	PRE-SERVE R 110	DUAL-STANDARD
REDUKT OR 1000	AUTOMATIK 2000	BRILLIANT 880 S
COMBI-PRO 80 C	DUOTRONIC 440	KONSEKUENT 64

protekt©
universal protection set

MODULAR 5533 I	PRE-SERVE R 110	DUAL-STANDARD
REDUKT OR 1000	AUTOMATIK 2000	BRILLIANT 880 S
COMBI-PRO 80 C	DUOTRONIC 440	KONSEKUENT 64

Sole Bag 2004

Naoto Fukasawa (Japanese, born 1956)
Rubber and canvas, 11 x 9½ x 3" (28 x 24 x 5 cm)
Manufacturer: Takara Co., Ltd., Japan (2005)

This canvas tote bag with a rubber sneaker sole is the creation of Japanese product designer Naoto Fukasawa for +-0 [read: "plus-minus-zero"], a design brand. As odd as it may seem, there is an advantage to having a tote bag with a sneaker sole: the bottom of the bag is protected from whatever might be on the floor or ground, whether it be dust, water, or dirt. This unlikely marriage between two familiar items results in a novel yet practical product and is a hall-

mark of Fukasawa, who is famous in Japan for his 1999 design of a wall-hung CD player with built-in speaker for the company Muji, which looks much like the kind of wall-mounted ventilation fan typically found in Japanese houses.

Fukasawa founded his Tokyo-based company in 2003. Prior to this, he headed the Japanese branch of IDEO, an American product-design firm based in Palo Alto that is known for its wide range of products, from the stand-up toothpaste tube to palm-held computers. His collaboration with Takara consists of a line of unique electronic appliances as well as everyday items, like the Sole Bag under the +-0 brand.   —H. Y.

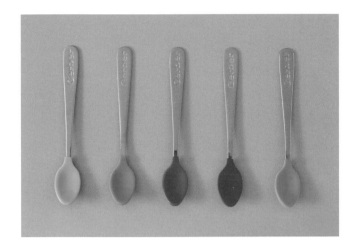

Infant Spoons, soft bite safety spoons n.d.

Gerber company design (USA, est. 1928)
Silicone and steel, 5 ½ x ⅞" (1.4 x 2.2 cm)
Manufacturer: Gerber Products Company, USA

Panda Door Pinch Guard 2001

Mommy's Helper company design (USA, est. 1986)
EVA foam
Manufacturer: Mommy's Helper, Inc., USA (2001)

Stokke Xplory baby stroller 2003

Bjørn Refsum (Norwegian, n.d.), Hilde Angelfoss Øxseth
(Norwegian, n.d.), K8 Industridesign (Norway, est. 1998), and
Bård Eker Industrial Design (Norway, est. 1994)
Aluminum, polyamide, and polyester,
45 ¾ (max.) x 22 ⅝ x 32" (116 max. x 58 x 75 cm) unfolded;
22 ⅝ x 16 ⅝ x 39" (58 x 42 x 99 cm) folded
Manufacturer: Stokke AS, Norway (2003)

"Children deserve a better view." This motto sums up
the main achievement of the Stokke Xplory, a baby
stroller designed with a high seat that gives a child
an overall perspective so he can experience everything that is going on, lifted away from city dust,
heat, and fumes. The child can also face his parents,
which reassures him, promotes stronger bonds, and
helps define the child's identity.

Stokke pays special attention to the active
nature of small children, providing solutions that let
them move around freely. The Xplory reincorporates
the philosophy of their celebrated KinderZeat—an
ergonomically designed chair introduced in 1972
that provides foot, leg, and back support for a child,
thus offering comfort and promoting proper development. An adjustable footrest gives the child a stable
base and enables him to alter postures. The angle of
the seat is also adjustable, from a sleep or rest position to active sitting.

Convenience for adults has been kept in mind
as well: the handle height and angle can be adjusted
to avoid back stress when pushing the stroller, and
the rear wheels are made of a unique rubber material filled with air bubbles that makes them softer and
prevents a flat tire. The Xplory stroller has been
designed around a central bar that acts as a spinal
cord, comprising a handle, a seat, a bag, and wheels,
which makes it easier to fold and store.   —P. J.

Body Props 2000

Olivier Peyricot (French, born 1969)
IDSland (France, est. 2000)
Polyurethane foam and fabric, various dimensions
Manufacturer: Edra S.p.A., Italy (2001)

The five Body Props—for neck, back, knees, elbows, and stomach—have been designed as an extension of the human body. Molded in expanded polyurethane, with either a varnish or fabric finish, these soft ergonomic forms support and underline different postures: laying on the ground, propped up on one elbow, or resting on the knees or comfortably on the back. A fifth piece, a comma-shaped mold, encourages a more personal use and opens up a wider range of possibilities. Like Olivier Peyricot's Vigilhome (see page 65), these props are an interpretation of the idea of comfort. By embracing the floor as a living space, Body Props help relieve strain on the spine and offer a sense of safety through permanent contact with the body. —P. J.

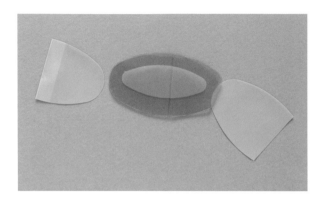

Band-Aid Advanced
Healing Blister 2001

Coloplast (Denmark, est. 1957)
Hydrocolloid gel, 1¼ x 2⅛" (3.2 x 5.4 cm)
Manufacturer: Johnson & Johnson, USA (2002)

Anyone who has spent a day walking around in new shoes can appreciate the need for blister protection. Coloplast, a Danish company specializing in healthcare products, first developed a special form of hydrocolloid—a substance that forms gel with water—called Compeed for ulcer dressing in hospitals. Then it used this substance in a more mundane version, sold in drugstores, for the treatment of common wounds, especially blisters. Johnson & Johnson purchased the invention, so now we can officially call it a Band-Aid.

Flexible and tapered at the edges, it conforms to the skin almost perfectly, like an artificial, hygienic, and soft scab. Its surface is waterproof and washable, so it can be left on for days at a time. It looks like a translucent sticky slug. Once it is applied to the blistered area, it draws the fluids from the injured skin and turns them into a padding gel. After a few days, when the band-aid is removed from the healed skin, a ghost of the absorbed blister remains impressed in the gel. This gel provides extra cushioning to help protect the blister from re-injury.   —R. L.

Compeed X-TREME Flex 2002

Jan Marcussen (Danish, born 1957)
Polyurethane and hydrocolloid adhesive
Manufacturer: Coloplast A/S, Denmark (2004)

Safe band-aids Prototype, 2004

Karim Rashid (Canadian, born Egypt 1960) for KNOW HIV/AIDS
Vinyl, gloss, and cardboard box, various dimensions

HIV/AIDS is the fastest-growing and most-widespread epidemic in the world, and the best-known way to combat it is through education. As part of the Knowing is Beautiful public-service ad campaign, Karim Rashid designed a proposal for a bandage that would encourage testing for these diseases. A distinctive bandage was created in several shapes for use on both arm- and finger-test sites, its design meant to be a badge of honor that could be worn proudly by the user. —R. L.

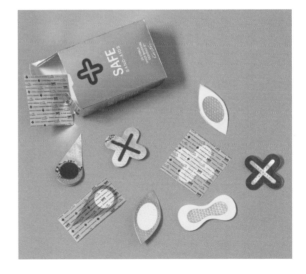

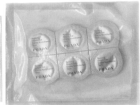

Monodose Skincare Cosmetics 2000

Karim Rashid (Canadian, born Egypt 1960)
Tyvek, acetate, polypropylene, polyethylene,
polyethylene terephthalate, and AL and EVOH plastics,
1⅝ x 2⅛" (4.1 x 5.3 cm)
Manufacturer: Prada Beauty, Italy (2000)

Crave Aid satiety patches Concept 2004

Thomas Overthun (German, born 1959), **Joanne Oliver** (New Zealander, born 1974), **Pontus Wahlgren** (Swedish, born 1974), **David Webster** (Scottish, born 1969), **Ian Groulx** (American, born 1973), and **Jared Mankelow** (New Zealander, born 1978) of **IDEO** (USA, est. 1978)
Steel and printed stickers, dispenser: 14 x 9⅜ x 3"
(35.5 x 24 x 7.5 cm)

Crave Aid was designed for the exhibition *Value-Meal: Design and (over)Eating*, organized by Aric Chen and Laetitia Wolff/futureflair for the Saint-Etienne International Design Biennal in November 2004. This conceptual piece about addiction was obviously inspired by the nicotine patch. However, instead of releasing chemicals as nicotine patches do, Crave Aid satiates unhealthy cravings through a placebo effect. Like first-aid kits, Crave Aid dispensers could be placed at different locations, providing emergency relief. With Crave Aid, IDEO lightheartedly comments on obesity and over-indulgence, serious and ever-growing issues in our present-day culture. —R. L.

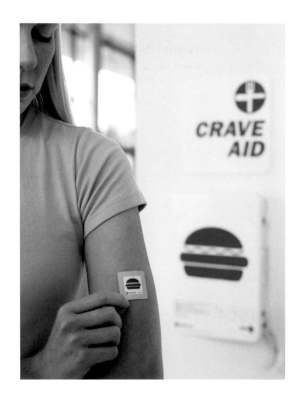

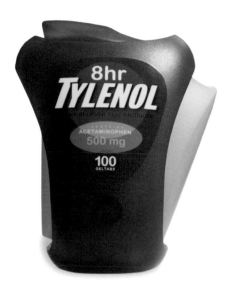

Tylenol Bottle Concept Prototype: 2004

Yves Béhar (Swiss, born 1967), **Eskil Tomozy** (Danish, born 1969), and **Johan Liden** (Swedish, born 1974) of **fuseproject** (USA, est. 1999)
Polyethylene, 3 ⅝ x 2 ¾" (9 x 7 cm)
Future manufacturer: Mc Neill-PPC, Inc., Consumer and Specialty Pharmaceuticals, a Johnson & Johnson company, USA (n.d.)

A common dilemma when designing a medicine bottle is how to make it easy enough for an adult to open, yet safeguard its contents from children. Béhar has developed such a bottle, which has a straighforward opening mechanism that can be easily "palmed" by the user and the pill container rotated into dispensing mode. This two-step operation meets child-safety requirements, while keeping each operation straightforward and tactile, even for arthritis patients. Another safety issue, pill identification, is addressed by the bottle's translucent surface, and the egg shape of the container suggests the structural integrity of this new design. —R. L.

The Corner-Cut Carton 2004

Kazuhiro Hiraishi (Japanese, born 1969)
Bravis International, Ltd. (Japan, est. 1996)
Corrugated paper, 16 x 10¾ x 5" (40.8 x 27.2 x 12.9 cm)
Manufacturer: Kirin Brewery Co., Ltd.
(Tokan Packaging System Co., Ltd.), Japan (2004)

Inflata-Pak Air Cushion Packaging 2000

3M company design (USA, est. 1902)
Heat-sealed nylon, 7¾ x 11¾" (19.6 x 29.8 cm);
inside pocket: 5 x 8" (12.7 x 20.3 cm)
Manufacturer: 3M, USA (discontinued 2000-2004)

BananaBunker 2000

Paul R. Stremple (American, born 1961) and
Margaret Breuker (American, born 1968) of
Cultured Containers (USA, est. 2001)
K-Resin styrene butadiene copolymer,
8 ¼ x 2 ¼" (30 x 6 cm)
Manufacturer: Rocheleau Tool & Die Co., Inc., USA (2005)

Urban

Canard

Vichy

Journal

Crazypack Cigarette Package Covers 2003-04

Sighild Blanc (French, born 1982),
Gauthier Guillet (French, born 1967), and
Frédéric Chatillon (French, born 1968)
Paper, height 2 ½ x 2 ¼ x ⅛" (6.3 x 5.6 x 2.3 cm) front;
height 3" (7.5 cm) back
Manufacturer: Dolmen, G&A prnc, France (2003-04)

Class 95 Particulate Respirator 1995

3M company design (USA, est. 1902)
Nonwoven microfibers, 3 ¼ x 8 ½ x ¾"
(8.3 x 21.6 x 1.8 cm) folded; 5 ⅛ x 4 ¾ x 3 ½"
(13 x 12 x 9 cm) unfolded
Manufacturer: 3M, USA (2004)

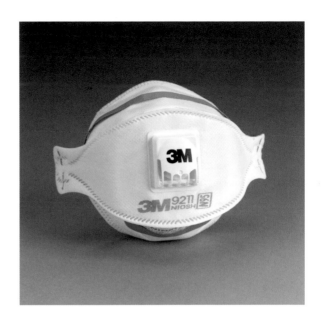

Clean Call disposable telephone covers 1993-94

Elizabeth A. Wilkes (American, born 1945)
Paper, 12 x 7 ½" (30.5 x 19 cm)
Manufacturer: Clean Call, USA (1995)

B Threwny Static Electricity Remover 2002

Kazuhisa Shimizu (Japanese, born 1966)
Acrylic resin, brass, synthetic rubber, and steel,
¾ x 2 ½ x ¼" (2 x 6.5 x 0.82 cm)
Manufacturer: Pentel Co., Ltd., Japan (2002)

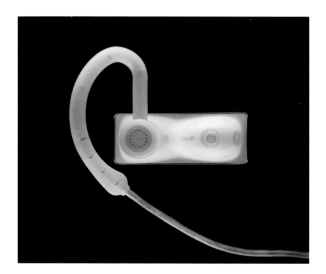

Aliph Jawbone Headset 2004

Yves Béhar (Swiss, born 1967)
fuseproject (USA, est. 1999)
ABS plastic, stainless steel, and elastomeric rubber,
2 x 2 x ½" (5 x 5 x 1.5 cm)
Manufacturer: Aliph, USA (2004)

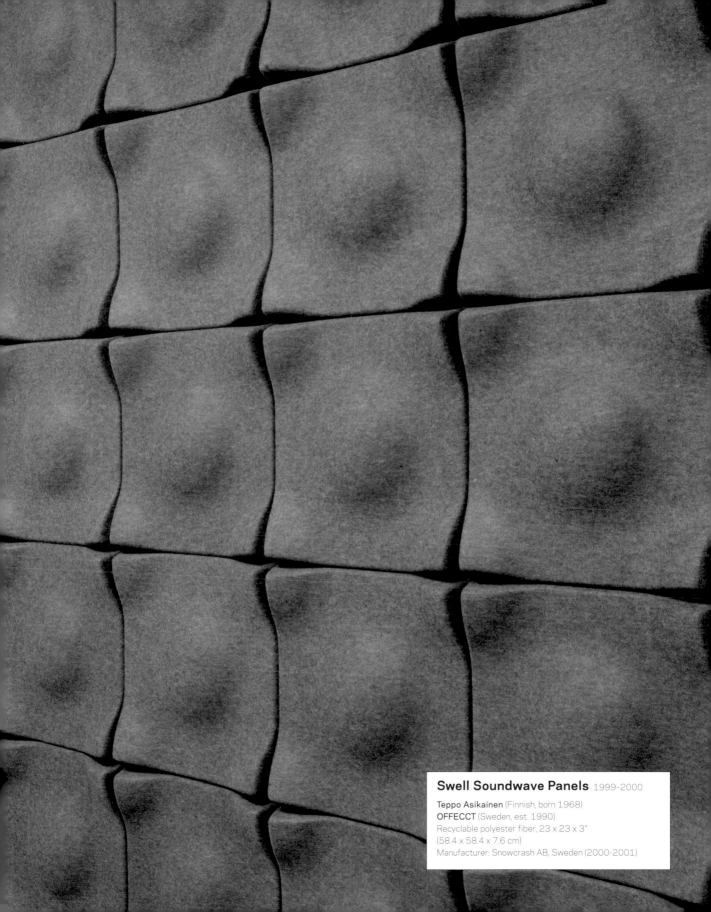

Swell Soundwave Panels 1999-2000

Teppo Asikainen (Finnish, born 1968)
OFFECCT (Sweden, est. 1990)
Recyclable polyester fiber, 23 x 23 x 3"
(58.4 x 58.4 x 7.6 cm)
Manufacturer: Snowcrash AB, Sweden (2000-2001)

Capsters Sports Headgear for Muslim Women, Tennis, Aerobics, and Outdoors versions 1999

Cindy van den Bremen (Dutch, born 1972)
Polyester, cotton, and fleece, respectively
Manufacturer: Capsters, The Netherlands (2001)

Raincoat n.d.

Local Industries of Güines (Cuba)
Recycled nylon sugar sack, 39 ⅜ x 59" (100 x 150 cm)
Manufacturer: Local Industries of Güines, Cuba

Watercone water-collection device 1999

Stephan Augustin (German, born 1967)
Makrolon polycarbonate, 11¾ x 31½"
(30 x 80 cm) diam.
Manufacturer: Wisser Verpackungen GmbH,
Germany (2004)

Shapla Arsenic Removal Filter 2001

Fakhrul Islam (Bangladeshi, born 1939)
International Development Enterprises
(Bangladesh, est. 1981)
Clay, plastic, cloth, and ferrous sulfate,
22 x 25" (56 x 63.5 cm) diam.
Manufacturer: Shapla Water Products, Bangladesh (2001)

Safe Sari 1996

Anwar Huq (American, born 1951) and
Rita Colwell (American, born 1934)
Cotton, folded four to eight times,
45 x 45" (114 x 114 cm)
Manufactured in Bangladesh (1996)

Ufocap umbrella 2003

Jae Bong Yang (Korean, n.d.)
PVC plastic
Manufacturer: Koryo Industrial Co., Ltd., Korea (2004)

mizu-Q Straw Water Purifier 1990

Yasuyuki Yamamoto (Japanese, born 1940)
Antibacterial polypropylene
Manufacturer: Meiko Co., Ltd., Japan (1990)

Patapata Pen Chan
water running warning 1997

Suruga company design (Japan, est. 1979)
Polystyrene and PVC
Manufacturer: Suruga Co., Ltd., Japan (1997)

Patapata Pen Chan, which means "Flapping Penguin" in Japanese, is a bathroom accessory that helps motivate Japanese children to learn safe hygiene habits. This plastic penguin flaps its wings whenever a toilet is flushed. Children love to see the animal in action, so they eagerly flush after using the toilet. Also, by taking advantage of a unique feature on many Japanese toilets, the Patapata Pen Chan helps children learn to wash their hands.

Most toilets in Japanese homes are tucked away in closet-sized locations that are often too small to accommodate washbasins. So, without sacrificing any precious space, Japanese designers have reshaped the tank lids on these toilets into small sinks. They have also extended the toilet's refill water pipe, which is usually hidden inside the tank of an American-style toilet, to the outside so water pours into the basin. When the toilet is flushed, fresh refill water comes out of this pipe, much like water from a sink faucet, and is available for hand washing before it drains through a small hole in the lid into the tank.

The Patapata Pen Chan attaches to the mouth of the refill water pipe. When the toilet is flushed, the refill water flows into the mechanism inside the penguin, causing its wings to flap exuberantly. For added fun, parents can put clear plastic or glass pebbles into the basin to simulate the icy setting of a penguin's home in Antarctica.   —H. Y.

Solo Traveler Plus re-closable hot cup lid 2003

Bryce G. Rutter (Canadian, born 1957), Brian Bone (Canadian, born 1963), and Heath Doty (American, born 1969) of Metaphase Design Group, Inc. (USA, est. 1991)
Polystyrene, 1 1/8 x 3 3/4" (3 x 9.5 cm)
Manufacturer: Solo Cup Company, USA (2004)

Java Jacket Cup Sleeve 1993

Jay D. Sorensen (American, born 1958)
Recycled paper, 11 x 2 1/2" (30 x 6.5 cm)
Manufacturer: Java Jacket, Inc. USA (1993)

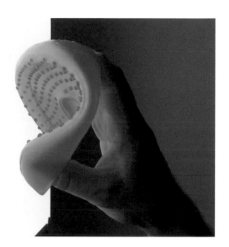

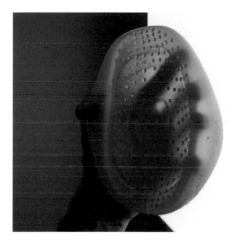

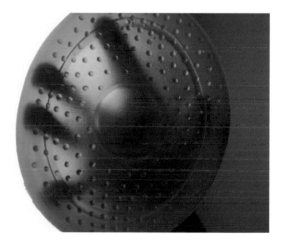

Too Hot to Handle Prototype. 2003

Duncan Turner (British, born 1979)
Silicone, 6 ½ x 5 ⅜ x 1 ⅝" (16.5 x 13.5 x 4 cm)

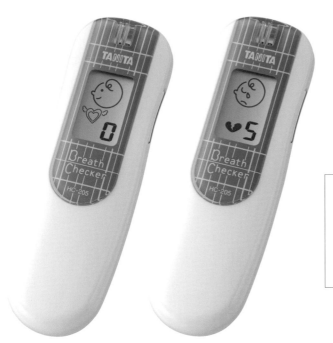

Fresh Kiss Breath Checker 2003

Tamaki Shoji (Japanese, born 1973),
Miwako Murase (Japanese, born 1973), and
Yoko Akai (Japanese, born 1973)
ABS plastic and acrylic resins, 3 ⅝ x 1 ¼ x ⅝"
(9.3 x 3.16 x 1.65 cm)
Manufacturer: Tanita Corporation, Japan (2004)

Smellkiller 1999

Dirk Zielonka (German, born 1965)
Stainless-steel alloy, 3" (7.6 cm) diam.;
base: 1¼ x 7 x 7" (3.1 x 17.7 x 17.7 cm)
Manufacturer: Zielonka CNC Dreh- und Frästechnik GmbH,
Germany (1999)

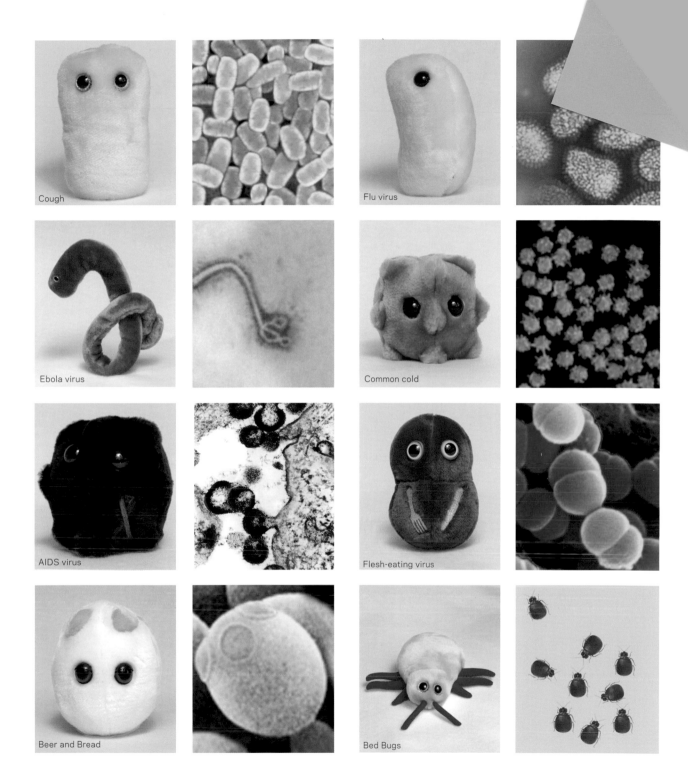

Cough

Flu virus

Ebola virus

Common cold

AIDS virus

Flesh-eating virus

Beer and Bread

Bed Bugs

GIANTmicrobes 2000

Andrew Oliver II (American, born 1970)
Polyester, each 5" (12.5 cm)
Manufacturer: Giantmicrobes, Inc., USA (2001)

The study of emergency equipment was the spark for this exhibition and catalogue, not surprisingly since objects designed for use in emergency situations are the epitome of good functional design. Conceived with efficiency and economy in mind, they must be as clean, sturdy, light, and intelligent as possible in order to minimize errors and ensure the well-being of both the person who uses them and, if such is the case, of the endangered person on whom they are used. Designers sometimes work with advanced materials and the latest technology, but even when they don't, their designs are easily understandable and deployable. They are nearly perfect, as perfect as a fire truck, an ambulance, or a Swiss army knife.

Emergency equipment often comes in compact kits to be kept at hand under a desk, in the trunk of a car, or in UN warehouses. Battery-operated radios and flashlights are also a staple of any emergency list. The International Red Cross sells many different types of preparedness kits suitable for different local conditions. The most common kits contain a generic supply of items for dressing wounds and stopping bleeding, but kits are becoming more and more specialized.

emergency

In areas prone to seismic activity, for instance, the population is used to storing extra water and food, as well as all-important personal records on an easily transportable CD. Sophisticated kits with assorted medicines, tongue blades, and emergency splints are easily found in convenience stores. In areas that suffer from moderate flooding, inhabitants often own inflatable barriers ready to be installed. There are also kits for mountain trekkers, workers in tall office buildings, car drivers, and even good Samaritans who want to be ready to perform an emergency tracheotomy with their key holder kit. Recently introduced was a home cardiac defibrillator, a streamlined version of the portable defibrillator that can be found in any airport or airplane.

Readiness and preparedness, two words commonly used in the United States after 2001, are a normal way of life in many parts of the world. Designers have added their touch by attempting to integrate preparedness in the landscape of everyday life, by concealing a compact emergency chamber under a table, for instance, which, in case of an earthquake and in the absence of better choices, becomes a preferred shelter. In Japan, a region of the world just waiting for yet another devastating earthquake, fire-resistant hoods are distributed to children as part of their standard school equipment. In Israel, where the entire population is equipped with gas masks to resist biochemical attacks, and tension is a way of life, designers have devised masks and respirators that allow for the most soothing human activities, such as having a soda or enabling a mother to hug her child. Grace under pressure is what design can provide. —P. A.

Feeding cup n.d.

Girl feeding her malnourished brother with the cup used
by Doctors Without Borders in the therapeutic feeding
center, Mornay, Darfur, Sudan, 2004

Water container n.d.

UNICEF United Nations Children's Fund (est. 1946)
PVC-coated polyester, polyethylene, or
equivalent materials. Collapsible, capacity 20 liters
Multiple manufacturers

The United Nations Children's Fund (UNICEF) was
established in 1946 to aid children around the world.
The organization provides a wide range of services,
from procuring basic necessities like food and cloth
ing to more extensive aid in the form of education
and housing to Third World and developing countries. Along with education about water sanitation,
UNICEF distributes this collapsible water container
to help combat the spread of diseases that strikes
many children living in unhygienic conditions. This
container is designed with built-in safeguards that
prevent water from being touched with one's hands
or being drunk directly from the container, thus keeping the water free from contamination and safe for
children.   —R. L.

**Prepare Oregon UNDERtheTABLE
Workstation Safety Kit** 2002

American Red Cross Oregon Trail Chapter (USA, est. 1917)
PETG plastic and vinyl, 6 x 4½" (15 x 11.5 cm) diam.
Manufacturer: Sinclair Rush, USA (2003)

**Lifestat Emergency
Pocket Airway** 1970

Ronald J. French (American, born 1938)
Stainless steel and aluminum, 3½ x ½" (15.24 x 1.27 cm)
Manufacturer: Prestige Products, USA (1996)

First-Aid Bag for the French Red Cross 2001

Frédéric Ruyant (French, born 1961)
Synthetic fiber, 10 ⅝ x 5 ⅛" (27 x 13 cm) diam.
Manufacturer: JPMA, France (2001)

The initiative for the conception of this first-aid bag came from the department of communications at the French Red Cross. The intention was to create a product that could be commercialized through an appealing, eye-catching design and make the message of the institution more timely and universal.

French architect Frédéric Ruyant got the inspiration for his *trousse d'urgence* from a Saint Bernard dog's barrel. The first-aid bag was launched with great fanfare in designer shops in 2001, before becoming a global item on the shelves of large department stores. To date, more than two hundred thousand bags have been sold.

The bag displays a reflective red cross and contains thirty-nine elements: a notepad and pencil, three plastic bags, a whistle, splinter tweezers, an elastic armband, a triangular sling, a bandage, a life blanket, two pairs of gloves, a pocket lamp, a pair of scissors, a dressing roll, twelve precut dressings, a compressive bandage, six compresses, an extensible band, a wound band, a roll of adhesive bandage, and a rain cape.

Another example of a first-aid kit, this one for the American Red Cross, is the UNDERtheTABLE Workstation Safety Kit (see opposite). Conceived to be stored under the office desk, to which it is attached with a loop-fastening device, and compact enough to take along in any emergency or when traveling, this tubular container includes a dust mask, a water pouch by SOS Food Labs, plus a whistle and a six-hour light stick manufactured by StarıSport.

—P. J.

HeartStart Onsite Defibrillator 2002

Kurt Fischer (American, born 1970)
Polycarbonate, ABS plastic, acrylic, and silicone,
7¼ x 8⅜ x 2⅞" (18.5 x 21 x 7 cm)
Manufacturer: Philips Medical Systems,
The Netherlands (2002)

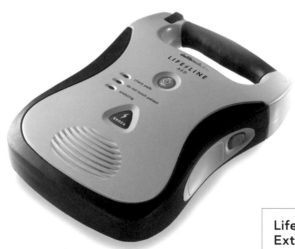

Lifeline AED Semiautomatic External Defibrillator 2002

Gintaras Vaisnys (American, born 1962), **Glenn Laub**
(American, born 1957), **Giovanni Meier** (American,
born 1963), **Matthew Callan** (American, born 1965),
Benny Chi (American, born 1962), and **Jim Sener**
(American, born 1961) of **Defibtech, LLC** (USA, est. 1999)
Polycarbonate, 8½ x 11¾ x 2¾" (22 x 30 x 7 cm)
Manufacturer: Defibtech, LLC, USA (2003)

Inflate-A-Shield CPR Barrier 1999

Andrew Serbinski (American, born 1949), Mark Rosen
(American, n.d.), and Mirazat Koć (Turkish, n.d.) of
Machineart (USA, est. 1988)
Jim Traut (American, born 1956) and Larry McKinney
(American, n.d) of Laerdal Medical Corporation Design and
Development Team (USA, est. 1967)
PVC, silicone, polypropylene, and 3M Filtrete bacterial filter
membrane, 2 ¾ x 2 ¾ x 2 ¾" (7 x 7 x 7 cm) folded
Manufacturer: Laerdal Medical Corporation, USA (2001)

DrägerMan PSS 500 Air Unit for firefighters 1998

Jakob Wagner (Danish, born 1963)
Carbon-infused polyamid, 21 ¼ 16 ½ x 13"
(54 x 42 x 33 cm)
Manufacturer: Dräger Safety AG & Co., Germany (1999)

Rescue Board 600 2001

Hiroyuki Tazawa (Japanese, born 1948)
Recycled paper, 29 x 71 x ⅛" (73.5 x 180 x 0.25 cm)
unfolded; 29 x 24 x ¼" (73.5 x 61 x 0.75 cm) folded
Manufacturer: Adachi Shiki Kogyo Co., Ltd., Japan (2001)

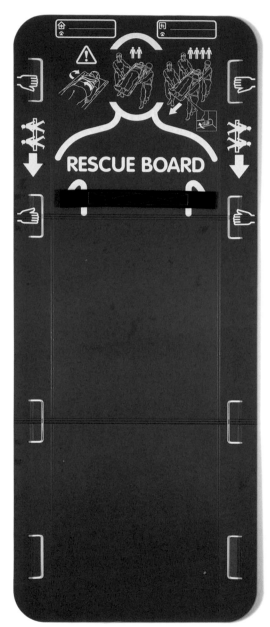

BaXstrap Spineboard 1997

Jim Traut (American, born 1956) and Mike Thomas (American, n.d.) of Laerdal Medical Corporation Design and Development Team (USA, est. 1967)
Polyethylene, carbon-fiber, and polyurethane foam, 16" x 6' x 2½" (40.6 x 182.9 x 6.3 cm)
Manufacturer: Laerdal Medical Corporation, USA (1997)

SAM Finger Splint 1984

Sam Scheinberg (American, born 1941)
EVA foam and O temper aluminum alloy, 1¾ x 3¾" (4.4 x 9.5 cm)
Manufacturer: Sam Medical Products, a division of The Seaberg Company, Inc., USA (1985)

3-in-1 Inflatable
Kite/Splint/Body Warmer c. 1990

Bernard William Hanning (British, born 1942) and
Vernon Pascoe (New Zealander, 1942-1999)
Mylar, 23' 11" x 29' 6½" (729 x 900 cm)
unfolded; 4 ¾ x 3 ½ x 1⅛" (12 x 9 x 3 cm) folded
Manufacturer: Skystreme UK, Ltd., UK (1997)

Blizzard Survival Bag 1998

Derek Ryden (British, born 1956)
Reflexcell, polypropylene, and rubber, 7' 4 ⁵⁄₈" x 67"
(225 x 170 cm) diam. unfolded; 8 ¼ x 4 ⅜ x 1 ⅛"
(21 x 11 x 3 cm) folded
Manufacturer: Blizzard Protection Systems, Ltd., UK (2003)

Radiation tent-jacket

Triage tent

Bio-hazard tent

Safety Gear for Small Animals 1993-ongoing

Bill Burns (Canadian, born 1956),
Museum of Safety Gear for Small Animals (Canada, est. 1994)
Various materials, about 25 items that fit inside a shoebox
Manufacturers: Dave Porter and Jackie Demchuk, Canada
(1994-2005)

This curious collection of Safety Gear for Small Animals (SGSA) is Bill Burns's ironic and, at times, humorous way of shedding light on serious ecological issues. His whimsical, man-made items for animals in the wild are meant to shock and intrigue onlookers. In the Victorian era, similarities between humans and animals were documented by science yet rejected by society, and these issues remain controversial today. With SGSA, Burns repopularized the subject, this time as an acceptable topic of discussion. He exploits the ridiculous to spark conversation about serious questions. Images in absurd scenarios—like a raccoon wearing a reflective vest or an otter with a gas mask—point out the need for more obtainable solutions to deforestation and an ever-expanding human population. This conceptual piece asks more questions than it answers and uses Burns's own mordant styling as a platform for discussing sensitive yet growing political, ecological, and social concerns.

—R. L.

Hardhat

Visor

Respirator

Safety vest

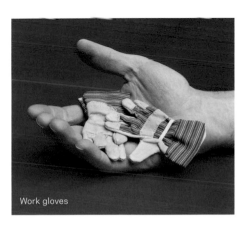

Work gloves

Mosquito net

Swiss Fondue
Earthquake Safety Table Prototype. 2001

École cantonale d'art de Lausanne (ECAL) (Switzerland, est. 1821)
Martino d'Esposito (Italian, born 1976)
Thermolacquered steel, 28¾ x 31½ x 47¼" (73 x 80 x 120 cm)

In 2001 students at the ECAL (École cantonale d'art de Lausanne) were invited to attend a workshop to develop a project on the subject of furniture that could be used in an emergency. This conceptual framework opened the discussion to functional and psychological issues, beyond formal concerns.

After a multidisciplinary exchange of ideas and a feasibility study of potential projects, student Martino d'Esposito's antiearthquake tables were chosen to represent the school at the *Salone Satellite* at the Milan Furniture Fair in 2001. His ironic approach to an emergency situation consists of two tables made of 3 mm red thermolacquered steel to be used in the event of an earthquake. One can crawl through the side openings to look for protection under the structurally reinforced tabletop. There a hidden survival kit is stored: a felt blanket, a shovel, two bottles of water, an emergency kit, an extinguisher, an oxygen mask, a plastic helmet, and an aluminum emergency blanket. Besides these basics, some special items are added, depending on three different interpretations of the design: the Swiss Fondue Table contains a fondue kit, a bottle of Swiss Saint-Saphorin white wine, a bottle of Kirsch, four forks, a ceramic pan, a lighter, a flashlight, and a Victorinox Swiss officer's knife; the Swiss Nostalgic Table includes a supplementary cuckoo clock, Toblerone chocolate, some dried fruits, a snowglobe, postcards, playing cards, three candles, and a ceramic plate; and the Adult Only version incorporates a porno magazine, whiskey, cigarettes, and a lubricant, suggesting some alternative activities in an emergency situation.   —P. J.

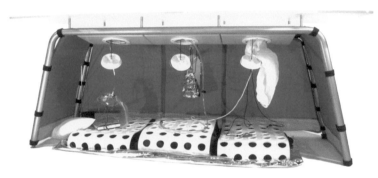

Undercover Table Prototype. 1999

Thom Faulders (American, born France 1961) and Anna Rainer (Swedish, born 1961) of Beige Design (USA, est. 1998)
Polycarbonate, steel, vinyl, and nylon, 29" x 30" x 6'
(73.5 x 76 x 183 cm)

The instinctive impulse to hide under a table during a natural or man-made disaster provided the idea for this Undercover Table, the collaboration of Thom Faulders and Anna Rainer, an architect and an artist, respectively, from the California-based studio Beige Design. The location of the studio and the awareness that at any time an earthquake can strike in California were defining factors in the origin of this project. The Undercover Table was designed in 1999 on the tenth anniversary of the Loma Prieta earthquake, which damaged a section of the Bay Bridge in San Francisco. This state of uncertainty encouraged them to rethink the items that surround us.

Their design transformed an everyday household table into a survival station. The table remains compact unless an emergency occurs, at which time a number of items pop up from the tanks beneath.

A typically unused and often forgotten space, the underpart of the table becomes the most significant element, both aesthetically and functionally. The storage tanks, oblong and brightly colored, are visible through the translucent polycarbonate top and are present at all times, like the latent threat, with an emergency kit ready to be deployed. The storage containers, which are held in place by perforated protective bands, can be detached from the bottom of the table and stuffed with soft items, thus providing a padded surface for reclining or sleeping. They can even be used as handbags, slings, or a soft helmet. The tabletop itself pulls off to be turned into a stretcher with handles. This unlimited resourcefulness is crucial in extreme situations, "requiring one to 'uncover' new functions for the world of things that surround us. The Undercover Table welcomes this spirit of invention," explain the designers. As an oasis in the midst of a possible catastrophe, it becomes "a house within a house," an example of micro-architecture created from a conventional piece of furniture. —P. J.

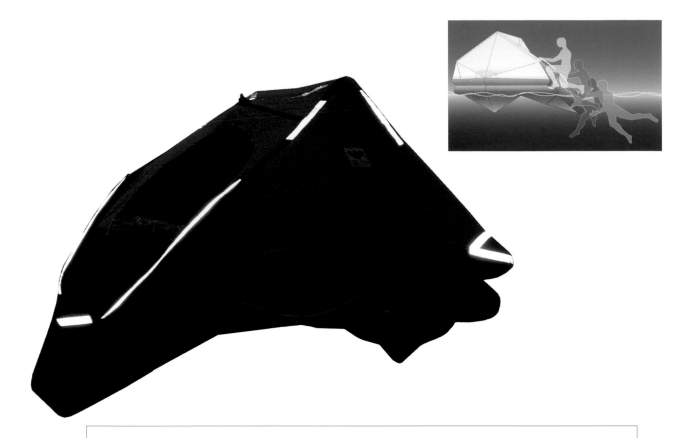

Sea Shelter 2004

Nikhil Garde (Danish, born 1972)
Designskolen Kolding (Denmark, est. 1967)
Instructors: **Elle-Mie Ejdrup Hansen** (Danish, born 1958),
Barnabas Wetton (British, born 1962), and **Michael
Frederiksen** (Danish, born 1966),
Viking Life-Saving Equipment (Denmark, est. 1960)
Nylon and rubber, 6' 6 ¾" x 10' 6" x 12' 1 ⅝"
(200 x 320 x 370 cm)
Manufacturer: Viking Life-Saving Equipment A/S,
Denmark (2004)

Sea Shelter is the graduation project of Nikhil Garde, a student at the Institute of Industrial Design and Interactive Media, Designskolen Kolding, in Denmark. It was carried out in cooperation with the maritime safety company Viking Life-Saving Equipment. Test studies of human interaction and behavior in life-threatening situations showed a need for a product that could be used readily at sea in extreme survival circumstances. The challenge in creating such a product required not only that it be flexible, lightweight, easy to launch, and self-righting, qualities that Viking's designs are noted for, but also that it be able to function in diminished physical conditions in the midst of a storm with strong winds and high waves.

In such a scenario, the most critical moment occurs when a person is attempting to board a life raft from the water. The design of this Viking raft takes into account this crucial factor: the need to properly balance one's weight when boarding. This raft, which is fitted with handles on either side at the back and a step that extends below the surface of the water, enables a person to grab the handles, place one knee on the step, and stretch out the leg. When the boarder achieves a synchronized balance with the raft, he is no longer vulnerable to the movement of the waves. From that position, he can then raise his legs from the water without putting strain on his arms, which are used only for stability. The wide step allows the occupants of the life raft to lean out to help other people coming in. The raft positions itself according to the direction of the wind and the waves, making the albeit extreme journey more comfortable, and can be oriented so that the opening to the raft faces toward people swimming to reach the Sea Shelter. —P. J.

Oscar Inflatable
Life Jacket 150N 2001

Helly Hansen company design (Norway, est. 1877)
Single chamber, Halkey-Roberts automatic inflation
valve, and PVC, 24 x 12" (61 x 30.5 cm)
Manufacturer: Helly Hansen ASA, Norway (2002)

NOAQ Tubewall
Flood Fighting System 1997

Sigurd Melin (Swedish, born 1952) and
Anders Mohss (Swedish, born 1958)
Reinforced PVC and polypropylene, 19 ¾" (50 cm) diam.
Manufacturer: NOAQ Flood Protection AB, Sweden (2005)

Personal SafetyVest 2002

Ed Kilduff (American, born 1970) and Dean Chapman
(British, born 1965) of Pollen Design (USA, est. 1997)
Paul Treible (American, born 1968) and Jon Leyfert
(American, born 1963) of Computer Design, Inc. (USA, est. 1988)
Manuel Saez (Argentinian, born 1973), Marc Plawner
(American, born 1974), and Erika Gerzsenyi (American, born
1972) of Humanscale Safety Products (USA, est. 1982)
Glass-filled PVC, 12 ½ x 8 ½ x 4 ½" (32 x 21.5 x 11.4 cm)
Manufacturer: Humanscale Safety Products, USA (2003)

The Personal SafetyKit is a comprehensive and personalized office evacuation system. The kit and its components are designed to be mounted under a desk and offer aid during an unexpected emergency. One of the versions of this kit, the Personal Safety-Vest, contains six tools: the Evac-U8 smoke hood, which allows a person to breathe for fifteen minutes in a smoke-filled room; a flashlight; a light stick; a locator alarm; and two preserved-water packets. Each item was chosen to give the wearer the ability to breathe, see, be seen, and be heard, all of which are vitally important in an evacuation situation.   —R. L.

High-Grade Protective Hood
for Emergency 2003

Debika Planning Room (Japan, est. 2000)
Acrylic and nylon, 11 ⅝ x 1 ⅜ x 19 ¼"
(29.5 x 3.5 x 49 cm)
Manufacturer: Debika Corporation, Japan (2003)

EVAC+ Emergency Escape
Smoke Hood 2002-03

John Swann (British, n.d.)
Ernest Kortschak (Canadian, n.d), Desmond Mayne
(Canadian, n.d.), Marcus Carius (Canadian, n.d.), and
Vicki Theriault (Canadian, n.d.) of EVAC+ Design/
Engineering Team (Canada, est. 2001)
Polycarbonate, ceramic catalyst, N-95 grade particulate
filter, and heat-resistant polyamide hood,
5¼ x 2¾" (13.5 x 7 cm)
Manufacturer: Brookdale International Systems, Inc.,
a DuPont Canada Company, Canada (2003)

Bazooka Joe Prototype. 2003

Ezri Tarazi (Israeli, born 1962)
**Industrial Design Department, Bezalel Academy of
Art and Design** (Israel, est. 1906)
Wool and stainless steel, 31½ x 27½ x ¾"
(80 x 70 x 2 cm)

SAFE includes a selection of the projects developed
by the students in the Industrial Design Department of
the Bezalel Academy of Art and Design in Jerusalem,
Israel, for the *Head Guard* exhibition of 2003 (see
page 82): Hamsa, evoking the traditional Jewish
amulet used for protection from the Evil Eye;
Shimonit; Mask (see opposite); and No Entrance.

In Bazooka Joe, a work by the head of the
Department, Ezri Tarazi, the filters and valves integrated in the pullover make it easy to switch from
everyday life to emergency mode.   —P. J.

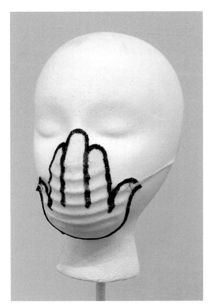

Shimonit Head Guard (upper left);
Mask Head Guard (above), **Hamsa Head Guard** (left) Prototypes. 2003, 1988, and 2003

Shimonit: **Michal Cohen** (Israeli, born 1978), **Omri Arif** (Israeli, born 1974), and **Yair Amishay** (Israeli, born 1970)
Wool, 9 7/8 x 7 1/8 x 9 7/8" (25 x 18 x 25 cm)

Mask: **Vered Kaminski** (Israeli, born 1953)
Stainless steel, 6 3/4 x 5 1/2 x 1/8" (17 x 14 x 0.2 cm)

Hamsa: **Ami Drach** (Israeli, born 1963) and **Dov Ganchrow** (American, born 1970)
Pressed paper, 6 3/4 x 4 x 1 1/8" (17 x 10 x 3 cm)

Industrial Design Department, Bezalel Academy of Art and Design (Israel, est. 1906)

**Mini Mamat Protection System
for Babies** (left) 1990

Bezalel Research & Development, Bezalel Academy of
Art and Design (Israel, est. 1906)
Polycarbonate and PVC laminate
Manufacturer: Shalon, Ltd., Israel (1991)

**Shmartaf Protection System
for Toddlers**
(opposite, top left and right) 1988-91

**Bardas Protection System
for Children** (opposite, bottom left) 1985-90

**Bardas Protection System
for Adults** (opposite, bottom right) 1985-90

Bezalel Research & Development, Bezalel Academy of
Art and Design (Israel, est. 1906)
Manufacturers: Shalon, Ltd., Superweld, Ltd., and
S.T. Safety Technologies, Israel (1991, 1990, and 1991)

Israel is the only country in the world where the entire population has the right, approved by Parliament, to be protected against chemical and biological warfare. Every Israeli citizen is given a protection kit that includes a sealed gas mask, which can be opened only when the Ministry of Defense gives official permission during an emergency. This nationwide plan covers all ages and ethnic groups.

Bezalel Research & Development, an initiative within the Bezalel Academy of Art and Design in Jerusalem, worked on a protection system whose main feature is an air blower that uses positive pressure inside the mask so that there is no need to breathe through the filter, making it easier for children and allowing some communication to take place.

Mini Mamat—the name comes from the initials MMT, meaning Protection Equipment for Infants—is designed for babies up to six months and consists of a transparent cell where the baby can lay down. The cell is connected to an air blower which pumps in filtered air (see above).

Shmartaf Toddlers Protection System—*shmartaf* is the slang word for babysitter in Hebrew—is a protective hood for children up to three years old. It covers the head, arms, and upper torso, and includes a milk-bottle accessory. It is suitable for fully active children who can walk, and the air blower unit can be attached to the child's back when moving around (see opposite). Most importantly, it allows full visual and tactile communication and interaction between mother and child.

Children Bardas—in Hebrew, *bardas* is a hood that covers the head—is a head-protection system for children aged two to eight years. The blower is tied around the child's waist, ensuring ease of movement and communication with the surroundings.

The Bardas system has also been developed for teenagers and adults. It covers the entire head, allowing a wider range of vision and better communication possibilities. The Bardas mask particularly suits male Orthodox Jews and Muslims whose beards prevented the regular rubber masks from being sealed. Adapting the blower solution from the Children Bardas, the masks were delivered to those who had beards because of religious beliefs as well as to patients with asthma or other breathing problems.

The protection system was used during the Gulf War, when some eight hundred thousand children had to wear the special protection units with the external air blower. Today, every newborn in Israel gets a free Shmartaf kit as an official gift from the government. —P. J.

Yaktrax Walker for icy conditions 1996

Thomas E. Noy (American, born 1948)
Thermoplastic elastomer and steel,
4 ½ x 6 ¾ x 4 ¼" (11.4 x 17.1 x 10.8 cm)
Manufacturer: Yaktrax, Inc., USA (1999)

AutoSock for snow 2002

Einar Hareide (Norwegian, born 1959) and **Anders Hansen**
(Norwegian, born 1971) of **Hareide Designmill**
(Norway, est. 2000)
Bård Løtveit (Norwegian, born 1959)
Polyester
Manufacturer: AutoSock AS, Norway (2002)

Snow Grabber 2001

Hiroyuki Tazawa (Japanese, born 1948)
Recycled paper, 8 x 22" (20 x 55 cm)
Manufacturer: Adachi Shiki Kogyo Co., Ltd., Japan (2001)

Startloop car battery starting device 2001

Einar Hareide (Norwegian, born 1959) and **Anders Hansen** (Norwegian, born 1971) of **Hareide Designmill** (Norway, est. 2000)
ABS plastic, 13 x 3 x 1⅝" (33 x 7.4 x 4 cm)
Manufacturer: Startloop AS, Norway (2001)

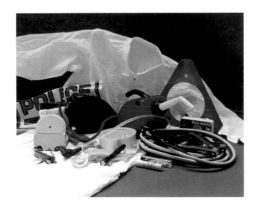

Emergency Safety Kit 1998

Dennis Carlson (American, born 1946)
Carlson Technology, Inc. (USA, est. 1982)
Various materials, 8 x 16" (20 x 40 cm) diam.
Manufacturer: McLaren Performance Technologies, Inc., USA (1999)

Adequate preparation for the unexpected can be vital in an emergency but is not always possible. The Safety Kit for Motorists stores all the necessary items for an unforeseen automobile-related emergency in the unused portion of a car's spare tire. The kit includes jumper cables, a one-gallon fuel can (with disposable bladders), an air compressor, a siphon pump (hand operated), a reflective warning triangle, a towing strap, a flashlight, three flares, a first-aid kit, fuses, a lock thaw, a Leatherman multi-purpose tool, latex gloves, protective coveralls, a police aid sign, handwipes, and a rag. It does not take up any of the car's trunk or passenger space. —R. L.

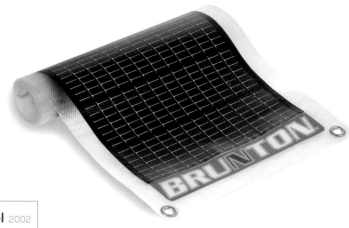

SolarRoll 14 Flexible Solar Panel 2002

Brunton company design (USA, est. 1894)
Amorphous solar cells and DuPont Tefzel fluoropolymer
film, 12 x 57" (30.5 x 144 cm) unrolled; 12 x 3"
(30.5 x 7.5 cm) rolled
Manufacturer: Brunton, USA (2003)

FreeCharge Mobile Phone Charger 2001

Barry Whitmill (South African, born 1970), **John
Hutchinson** (South African, born 1952), **Pierre Becker**
(South African, born 1970), **Stefan Zwahlen** (South
African, born 1957), **Jonathan Sables** (South African,
born 1975), and **Mark Marshall** (South African, born 1965)
of **Freeplay Energy Plc.** (South Africa, est. 1996)
Glass-filled nylon, ABS plastic, acetal, polycarbonate, stain-
less steel, and brass, 2 x 5 1/4 x 2 3/8" (5.2 x 13.5 x 6 cm)
Manufacturers: Freeplay Energy Plc., South Africa, and
Motorola, Inc., USA (2001)

FPR2 Human Powered Radio 1998

Roelf Mulder (South African, born 1959), Byron Qually
(South African, born 1973), and Etienne Rijkheer
(South African, born 1949) of ...XYZ Dot Dot Dot
Ex Why Zed Design, Ltd. (South Africa, est. 2000)
Polycarbonate, ABS plastic, nylon, and brass,
7 ⅞ x 11 x 7 ¼" (20 x 28 x 18.5 cm)
Manufacturer: Freeplay Energy Plc., South Africa (1998)

Freeplay focuses on the development of a self-suffi-cient energy system based on the storage of human mechanical effort to be delivered as electricity when needed. A carbon steel spring stores the energy generated by winding a handle. The energy is converted into electricity, charging the battery that powers the device. This renewable and ecological energy can either be applied to specific products, such as radios and flashlights, or be a stand-alone unit able to power several devices, including computers and medical equipment. Together with the designers of ...XYZ, Freeplay has developed a human-powered radio that does not require batteries (above). In a large-scale emergency, when communications and infrastructures are down, this radio can provide an efficient way of reaching a large number of people and keeping them aware of the situation.

A more robust and colorful version, the Lifeline radio (see page 11), has been conceived to operate in the harshest conditions and climates. The Freeplay Foundation, a humanitarian organization that works mostly in Africa, distributes the self-powered Lifeline radio to distant communities that have no access to electricity or batteries. The greatest obstacle to the alleviation of poverty is isolation. Radio can play a vital and even life-saving role in its capacity to reach anyone isolated by geography, conflict, or illiteracy, giving them access to information and education.

Freeplay has also designed an emergency lantern and a mobile phone charger (see opposite). The FreeCharge energy pack for a cell phone offers two power sources: an internal rechargeable battery and a wind-up option for power supply at any time. The human-powered capability of these solutions makes them particularly suitable for disaster relief. This closeness to the basics that developing countries still preserve can become very helpful in unexpected emergency situations. —P. J.

Information, when clear and understandable, can provide a measure of safety. Awareness, knowing what to expect, is synonymous with being safe. This chapter deals with the fear of the unexpected, the need to monitor information and use it effectively, and the danger of misunderstanding instructions in crucial situations. Included here are such diverse products as the Corporate Fallout Detector, which informs customers at the supermarket of the ethical record of the companies that manufacture the products for sale in the aisles, airline-safety briefing cards, and night lights for children.

The need for clear communication between people and objects has increasingly become the responsibility of designers and engineers. The medical profession, for example, which in the past was considered so arcane as to be incomprehensible to common mortals, is today attempting to provide straightforward communication based on clear visual information. In the past few years, several designers have focused especially on medicines and patients, repositioning labels on prescription bottles for easier reading, for example, or creating a medication organizer that reminds patients when they need to take their drugs. Communication design covers both high and low technology. We have chosen to focus on technologies already in use rather than to delve into the realm of the possible but improbable. The emphasis is on the way information comes to us rather than the technology involved in presenting that information. Acoustic or verbal communication from a distance, whether it be a foghorn, an alarm phone on the subway tracks, or a cell phone for toddlers, must reach the recipient in a clear and understandable manner. Similarly, graphic design of safety instructions or of harm-reduction campaigns is effective only if the content is directly and efficiently presented.

awareness

Awareness requires the power to see clearly, to conquer the fear of darkness and of the unknown. This fear is best represented by children and the numerous night lights that have been designed for them, but it can then extend to examples of reflective gear that Scandinavian countries are particularly versed in because of the need to survive the darkness of winter. On the other hand, awareness often comes at the price of a certain loss of innocence. Surveillance, for instance, is a double-edged sword. Cameras are meant to protect us, but need to invade our privacy to do so.

The last pages are devoted to one of the most pressing problems in today's world: land mines. The staggering data about the number of unmapped mines and the number of people who die or remain mutilated every year call not only for better, lighter equipment to defuse these mines, but also for the prompt deployment of low-cost, easy-to-use detectors that various countries can afford and people can operate without difficulty. That is an awareness we not only welcome, but also urgently need. —P. A.

Corporate Fallout Detector

Prototype. 2004

James Patten (American, born 1977)
Steel, aluminum, rubber, and barcode scanner,
5¾ x 9½ x 10½" (14.6 x 24.1 x 26.7 cm)
Prototype by MIT Media Lab, USA (2004)

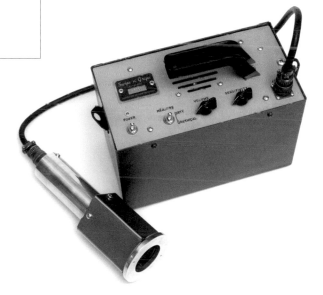

Securitree Prototype. 2004

Raúl Cárdenas Osuna (Mexican, born 1969)
Torolab (Mexico, est. 1995)
Steel, 57" x 57" x 7' 3" (152 x 152 x 221 cm)
Prototype by Bernardo Gutiérrez and Ana Martínez,
Mexico (2004)

Constant surveillance was once a subject reserved for science-fiction novels, but Raúl Cárdenas Osuna, founder of Torolab, a consortium of artists, designers, architects, and musicians based in Tijuana, Mexico, has brought to light the reality of ubiquitous and perennial tracking. Torolab developed the Securitree after studying the privileged urban conditions in San José and comparing them to those in Tijuana, located just twenty minutes south of the border with the United States. This work is a proposal for social change rather than a protest of current living conditions in certain areas. The comparison raised some obvious questions: What elements of privacy do we sacrifice in order to remain safe? What are people willing to compromise in order to live in a place like San José?

The Securitree is a two-part project consisting of a Transmitter Tree, with branches of cameras recording images of people on the street and relaying those images to the Receiver Tree, which is equipped with screens for viewing. When this piece was displayed as part of a solo exhibition, it was accompanied by photographic images of police occupation in San José, and a collection of writings on postmodern theories of utopian-like societies, including George Orwell's book *1984*. Visitors to the gallery became part of the exhibition unknowingly, through the Securitree transmitter, and willingly, through their participation in the Securitree Map. The idea behind the map was to allow the public to create its own cognitive map, placing stickers over areas of the city it identifies with violence, the police, wealth, and health. Identifying these issues central to their well-being helped to focus the discussion about improving the living conditions in Tijuana.

—R. L.

Life-Saving Station 1999

Peter Mortensen (Danish, born 1954), Eva Jarl Hansen
(Danish, born 1960), Gunner Hansen (Danish, born 1951),
and Torben Bregenhøj (Danish, born 1943) of
BBP Arkitekter (Denmark, est. 1992)
Birch plywood, 31' 2" x 11' 2 ⅝" x 8' ½"
(950 x 342 x 245 cm)
Manufacturer: Jönsson A/S, Denmark (2000)

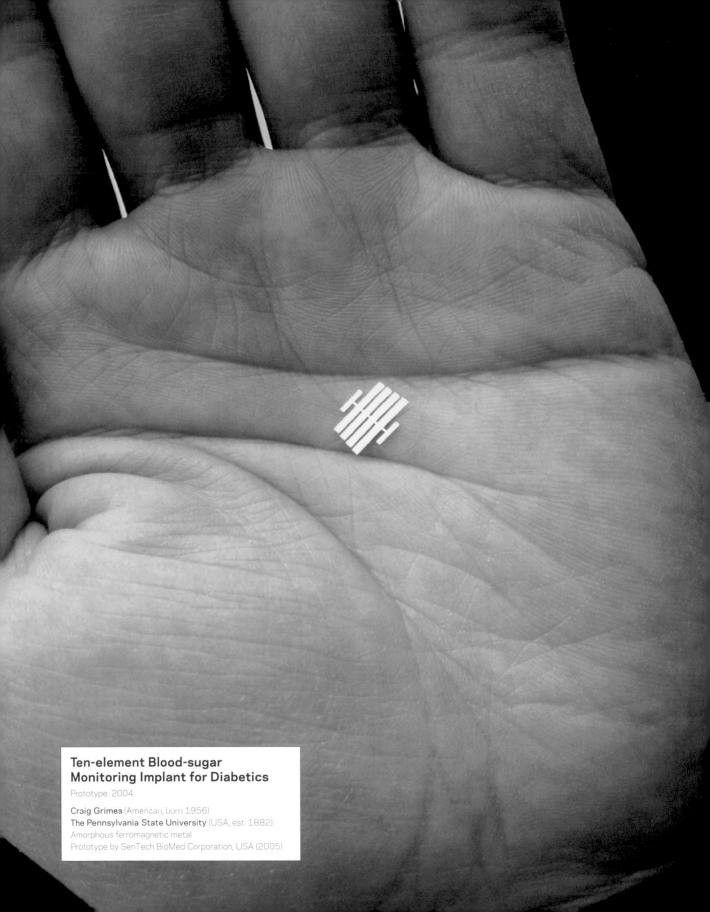

**Ten-element Blood-sugar
Monitoring Implant for Diabetics**

Prototype. 2004

Craig Grimes (American, born 1956)
The Pennsylvania State University (USA, est. 1882)
Amorphous ferromagnetic metal
Prototype by SenTech BioMed Corporation, USA (2005)

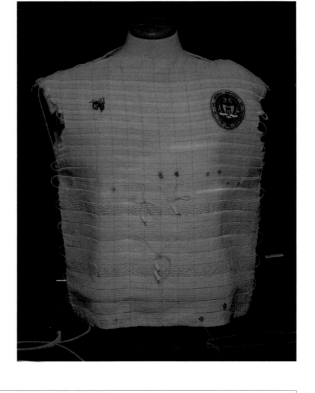

Georgia Tech
Wearable Motherboard Prototype, 1999

Sundaresan Jayaraman (American, born 1954), **Sungmee Park** (American, born 1964), and **Rangaswamy Rajamanickam** (Indian, born 1964) of **Georgia Institute of Technology** (USA, est. 1885)
Cotton, spandex, and conductive fibers,
22 x 16" (55.9 x 40.6 cm)

The loss of even a single soldier in war can alter the nation's engagement strategy, making it all the more important to save lives. The Wearable Motherboard was designed as a means to save time and lives in a combat situation. The Motherboard shirt has built-in sensors that are attached to the soldier's body and to a Personal Status Monitor (PSM)

worn at hip level. The Motherboard is activated when there is a break in the circuit, signifying a bullet wound. The PSM records the vital signs of the soldier and relays the information to an on-site medical triage unit. With this data, the medics can assess the seriousness of the injuries and respond accordingly.

This technology has enormous potential for civilian use as well. The lightweight shirt can be comfortably worn by anyone and can also be used to monitor patients in postoperative recovery or infants with respiratory problems, as well as astronauts, athletes, and law-enforcement personnel. In addition to the Wearable Motherboard, Georgia Institute of Technology has developed ideas related to wearable computing, robotics, and RNA research.   —R. L.

Bracelet of Life, Middle Upper Arm Circumference (MUAC) measuring device 1994

Médecins Sans Frontières (Doctors Without Borders)
(est. 1971)
Polypropylene, 12 ¾ x ¾" (32.4 x 1.9 cm)
Manufacturer: Trapinex Serigraphie-Offset, France (1994)

One-Day-At-A-Time Weekly Medication Organizer Tray 1990

Terry Noble (American, born 1945)
Polypropylene and polystyrene, ½ x 5 x 8"
(1.3 x 12.7 x 20.3 cm)
Manufacturer: Apothecary Products, Inc., USA (1990)

The Middle Upper Arm Circumference (MUAC) is a tool used in the field by volunteers of Médecins Sans Frontières (Doctors Without Borders) Commonly called the Bracelet of Life, this strip of plastic relays vital information about the health of a child (see opposite). In the poor parts of the planet, where mal nutrition is the chief cause of child mortality, it is important to identify high-risk cases of acute malnutrition as quickly as possible. This color-coded tool can be used by any language group to diagnose the severity of malnutrition in children ages six months to five years. The band is wrapped around the child's upper left arm. The circumference of the arm corresponds to a color, ranging from green (normal), to orange (moderate malnutrition), to red (serious malnutrition and risk of death). The Bracelet of Life Campaign began in 1998 to highlight the devastating famine in Sudan, brought on by years of warfare and drought. Since its use in volunteer organiza-

tions, the MUAC has helped to save many children.

In addition to aiding in the fight against malnutrition, Doctor Without Borders is committed to helping with the AIDS crisis in Africa. The most effective treatment for AIDS is the "drug cocktail," a specific combination of drugs that needs to be taken everyday at certain times. The One-Day-At-A-Time Weekly Medication Organizer Tray for HIV/AIDS medication (see above) is a tool that volunteers with Doctors Without Borders use to teach patients when to take their medication to ensure the effectiveness of the "cocktail."

This medication planner contains seven separate snap-out pill reminders, one for each day of the week, so patients can separate the corresponding box for that day and take it with them. Each daily pill reminder contains four compartments to help organize medications, making it easy to remember to take the necessary dosage. With the pocket-size organizer, patients can see at a glance if they have taken their dose.

—R. L.

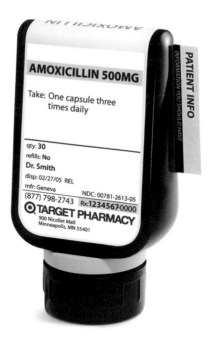

AMOXICILLIN

AMOXICILLIN 500MG

Take: One capsule three
times daily

qty: **30**
refills: **No**
Dr. Smith
disp: 02/27/05 REL
mfr: Geneva

NDC: 00781-2613-05
Rx:**1234567-0000**

(877) 798-2743

⊙ TARGET PHARMACY
900 Nicollet Mall
Minneapolis, MN 55401

PATIENT INFO

INFORMATION YOU SHOULD HAVE

Target ClearRx
prescription system 2004

Deborah Adler (American, born 1975) and
Klaus Rosburg (German, born 1962)
Polyethylene terephthalate, 2 ¼ x 4 x 1 ½"
(5.8 x 10.2 x 3.8 cm)
Manufacturer: Setco, Inc.,
a division of Kerr Group, Inc., USA (2005)

ClearRx is an innovative system that helps one read and understand the medical information that appears on a prescription bottle. The intention is to minimize confusion and mistakes in the use of medications prescribed by the physician, thus avoiding the misreading of dosage or taking another family member's medication. In fact, the idea for the new system started when designer Deborah Adler's grandmother took her husband's medication by mistake, and didn't realize until she started feeling sick. A recent survey revealed that sixty percent of adults have taken prescription medications incorrectly.

The bottle is designed so that there is a flat surface for the label, which wraps over the top of the bottle, while the cap is placed on the bottom. The pharmacy logo has been moved to the cap, where it does not block the prescription information. The shape of the bottle allows for easy gripping and opening, and all the vital facts are on the front panel, in the palm of the hand. This avoids having to turn the bottle to read the whole label. The patient can see everything at a glance. Prescription information has been hierarchically reorganized, with the drug name and dosage instructions at the top of the label. Each household member is assigned a color ring placed on the neck of the bottle, so the color code helps identify each person's medication. User-friendly icons have been created for the flat back surface of the bottle, clearly communicating health warnings.

Finally, a removable card inserted in a permanent sleeve on the ClearRx bottle contains important facts and side effects of the medication. The card has also been redesigned, summarizing essential information that was normally stapled to the pharmacy bag and that ninety percent of the time ends up in the trash can. —P. J.

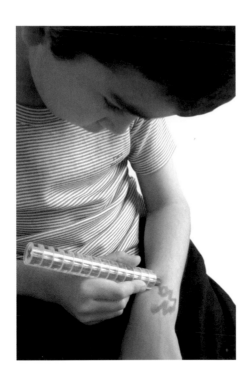

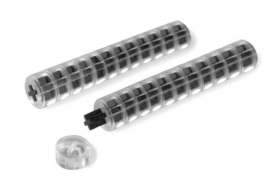

Therapeutic Felt-tip Pen Model. 2001

Mathieu Lehanneur (French, born 1974)
Various materials, 1⅛ x 1⅛ x 6" (3 x 3 x 15 cm)

The magic of treating illnesses vanished with the disappearance of apothecaries and healers. As the chemical composition of drugs grows in complexity, the emotional implications of its interaction with the patient are often forgotten. In Mathieu Lehanneur's mind, the restoration of the rituals associated with medication will retrieve the promise of healing.

Taking into account the patient's psychology, Lehanneur defines four kinds of relationship with a disease, based on feelings of repulsion, attraction, fear, or desire: the conflict, the coexistence, the refusal, and the imaginary illness. His series of Objets Thérapeutiques results from these states of mind (see pages 183–85).

The first category, the Conflictual relationship, deals with the perception of the illness as a threatening entity and the medication as the reminder of that menace. A transdermal analgesic for chronic pain, the Therapeutic Felt-tip Pen lets the patient write on the painful area of the body. The used cartridge is removed at the end of the day. The medicine disappears with the disease, until the patient gets to the final dose that represents his recovery.

In the Coexistence situation, a sort of nonaggression pact between the patient and his illness, he accepts the disease and an often lengthy treatment. The medicine becomes an integral part of the patient's everyday life, merging with his domestic rituals and habits. The First Mouthful is attached to the prongs of a fork when the medicine has to be taken orally at mealtime. A small dose of medication has been integrated into the Therapeutic Handkerchief, administered through the nose to alleviate allergic rhinitis.

In the Refusal relationship, the patient refuses to accept a real disease and the need for treatment, particularly when the symptoms seem nonexistent or the prescription is just preventive. Mutual dependence is emphasized in The Third Lung, a treatment for asthmatic patients in denial. In this case the medication is, in fact, the dependent, increasing its volume to alert the patient to the urgency of taking the dose to help it return to its normal shape. Liquid Bone is a cure for osteoporosis that renders visible an invisible pathology by gradually dissolving by effervescence, thus making evident the urgency of a remedy.

The concept of medication as an object in its own right, and the consideration of the patient's behavior as an integral part of the treatment will help establish new therapeutic solutions that integrate the emotional response and the daily ritual that it entails. —P. J.

The First Mouthful Model. 2001

Mathieu Lehanneur (French, born 1974)
Various materials, two pieces: ⅜ x 5⅛ x 7"
(1 x 13 x 18 cm) and ¾ x ¾ x 3⅛" (2 x 2 x 8 cm)

Therapeutic Handkerchief Model. 2001

Mathieu Lehanneur (French, born 1974)
Various materials, ⅜ x 2¾ x 2⅛"
(1 x 7 x 5.5 cm) folded

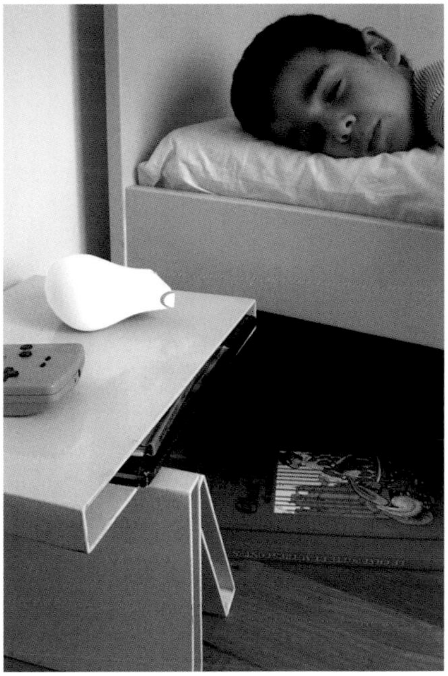

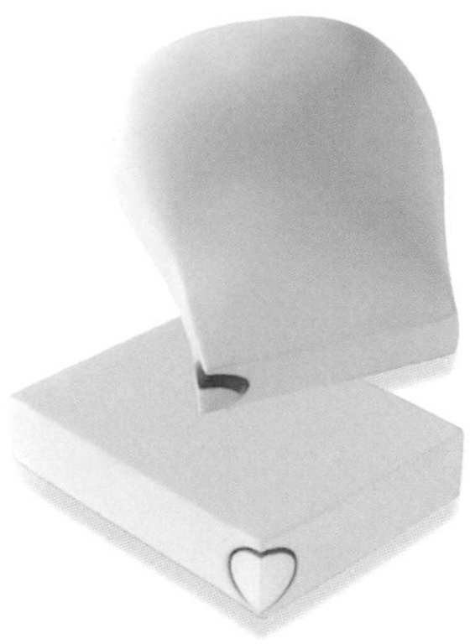

The Third Lung Model. 2001

Mathieu Lehanneur (French, born 1974)
Various materials, two pieces: $2\frac{3}{8} \times 3\frac{1}{2} \times 4\frac{3}{8}$"
($6 \times 9 \times 11$ cm) and $\frac{3}{4} \times 3\frac{3}{8} \times 2\frac{1}{2}$" ($2 \times 8.5 \times 6.5$ cm)

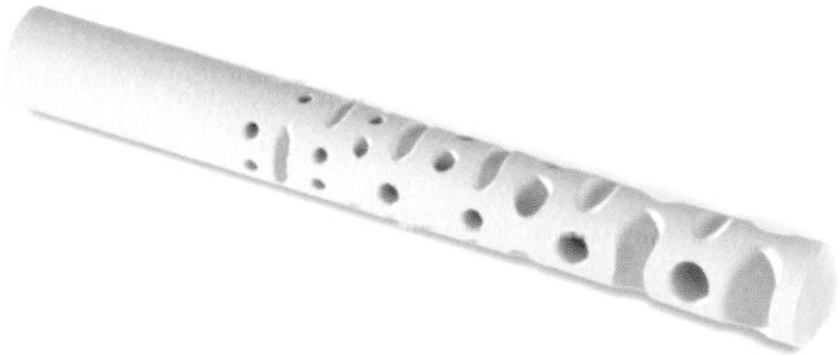

Liquid Bone Model. 2001

Mathieu Lehanneur (French, born 1974)
Various materials, two pieces: $\frac{3}{8} \times \frac{3}{8} \times 3\frac{1}{8}$"
($1 \times 1 \times 8$ cm) and $\frac{3}{4} \times \frac{3}{4} \times 3\frac{1}{8}$" ($2 \times 2 \times 8$ cm)

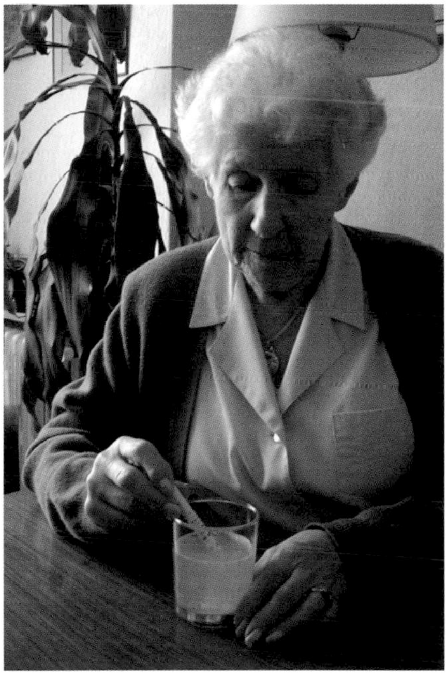

SBC SC605 In-Touch
Address Recorder 2002

Stéphanie Cobigo (French, born 1970) and
Stephen Heath (British, born 1969) of
Philips Design (The Netherlands, est. 1925)
Plastic and rubber, 2 x 1½ x ¾" (5 x 4 x 2 cm)
Manufacturer: Koninklijke Philips Electronics N.V.,
The Netherlands (2003)

Storm All-Weather Safety Whistle 1991

Howard Wright (American, born 1956)
ABS plastic, 2¾ x 1¾ x ⅞" (7 x 4.5 x 2.2 cm)
Manufacturer: Koller-Craft Manufacturing, Inc., USA (1991)

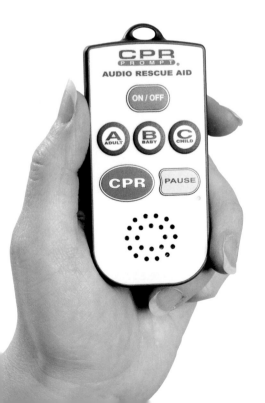

CPR Prompt Rescue Aid 1984

Donald Hutchins (American, n.d)
Plastic and electronic components,
3½ x 1½ x ¾" (9 x 4 x 1.3 cm)
Manufacturer: Nasco, USA (1984)

Help Point Intercom for the New York City Subway 2004

Masamichi Udagawa (Japanese, born 1964) and
Sigi Moeslinger (Austrian, born 1968) of
Antenna Design (USA, est. 1997)
MTA New York City Transit Team (USA, est. 1953)
Polycarbonate and LED light, and stainless steel,
64 ¾ x 7 ¾ x 7 ⅛" (164.5 x 19.6 x 18.1 cm)
Manufacturer: Siemens Transportation Systems, Inc., USA (2005)

The Metropolitan Transportation Authority (MTA) commissioned Antenna Design to develop an intercom system that would aid in relaying travel and emergency information in the subway. The current intercom system is not designed to provide travel information, leaving tourists to rely solely on subway maps for navigation. In cases of emergency, it connects only to the token booth and not directly to the fire dispatch. The integrated microphone and speaker in the new Help Point Intercom make it possible to contact security personnel twenty-four hours a day, seven days a week, and the more compact design is less prone to vandalism and breakage. Antenna Design has incorporated a blue LED into its intercom, in an attempt to provide a sense of safety and security in a manner that is not obtrusive during everyday activities, but is recognizable in an emergency. —R. L.

China Telecom Kid Mobile Phone

Prototype. 2003

Youngmihn Kim (Korean, born 1966) and
Seunghee Oh (Korean, born 1970) of
Design Continuum Seoul (Korea, est. 1983)
Injection-molded ABS plastic and electronic components,
1 ⅞ x 3 ½ x ¾" (4.7 x 8.9 x 2 cm)

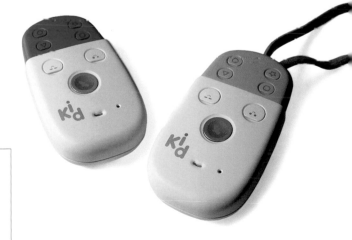

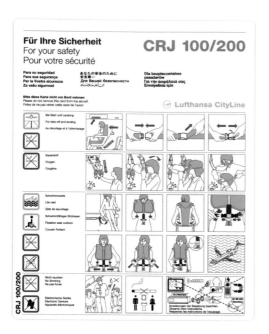
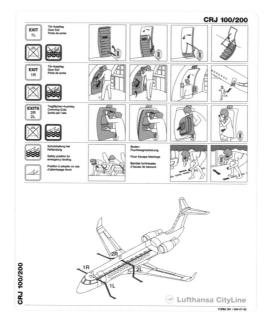

Lufthansa CityLine Passenger Briefing Cards for CRJ 100/200

Passenger Briefing Cards, more commonly known as Safety Cards, remind us of the risk we are taking whenever we board an airplane. That is exactly the purpose of the cards, and looking them over can make a big difference in an emergency. A 1974 study by the National Transportation Safety Board found that in an actual accident involving a wide-body jet, more than half of the passengers who did not read the cards were injured during the evacuation, while only one-sixth of those who did read them were.

Although no one seems to know who invented the first one, such safety brochures existed even in the early 1930s during the infancy of air travel. Those early cards were wordy and often had very few pictures. Even a card explaining how to don a cumbersome-looking life vest might only have a single drawing accompanied by an apologetic explanation starting with, "You are unlikely ever to need to wear one, but..."

To be certified, today's airlines are required by the Federal Aviation Administration (FAA) to provide oral or audio-visual preflight safety instructions to each passenger and to place them within easy reach, even though they have become so routine that passengers hardly pay any attention to them.

The cards must clearly explain the take-off and landing procedures for passengers, the locations and operations of exit doors, and the use of emergency equipment unique to each aircraft type and configuration. To be understood by everyone on board, it is required that the cards use photographs or illustrations and universally recognizable safety symbols, like the no-smoking sign with the slash over a cigarette inside a circle. The illustrations shown here exemplify the standard Passenger Briefing Cards with their simple drawings and symbols accompanied by as few written words as possible. Like aviation authorities in other countries, the FAA also recommends that the designs of the cards "be interesting and attractive so passengers will want to read them." Some of the most recent cards use everything from video-gamelike graphics to cartoons to attract passengers' attention.

There are several companies that specialize in designing Passenger Briefing Cards in the U.S. and Canada. The biggest challenge that card designers face is human nature rather than accidents. As an FAA advisory to the airlines says, "Motivating people, even when their own personal safety is involved, is not easy." —H. Y.

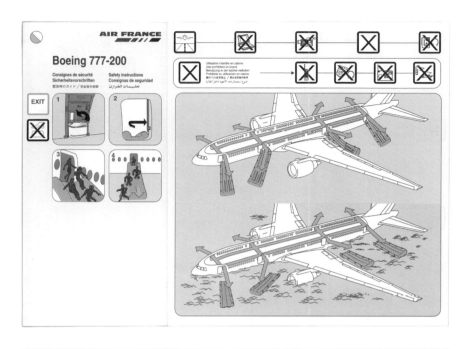

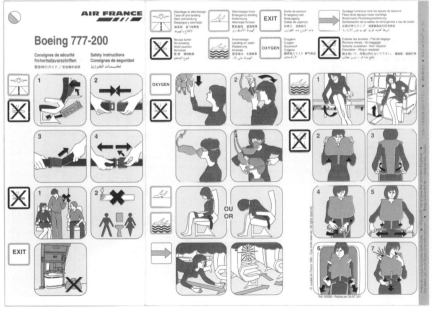

Air France Passenger Briefing Cards for Boeing 777-200

Visual instructions help us solve the most basic problems that we encounter every day. We may not even realize how much we depend on them.

Products do not speak for themselves, so designers and illustrators must create a visual language to give us directions when utilizing something for the first time, or deliver signs to help us find our way. The language of user instructions remains very primitive and has to be capable of reaching a wide audience. A limited number of signs and words enable us to handle all sorts of situations: from how to use the remote control or prepare our coffee in the morning, to how to operate a fire extinguisher or escape a building in an emergency.

Paul Mijksenaar and Piet Westendorp, both of whom are affiliated with the Department of Design at the Technical University of Delft in the Netherlands, have gathered a vast collection of user instructions. A number of these so-called mental maps and manuals have been reproduced in their book *OPEN HERE: The Art of Instructional Design* (1999). They collected these instructions from household and electronic appliances manuals, cut them from packages, scanned them from museum and company archives, or even bought them in thrift stores.

Mijksenaar is the principal of Bureau Mijksenaar, a design studio with offices in Amsterdam and New York that specializes in visual information design. Among his most recent projects are the Amsterdam Airport Schiphol information system, wayfinding for the Port Authority of New York and New Jersey PATH, and the new signage system for the New York area's three major airports: John F. Kennedy, Newark, and LaGuardia. —P. J.

IKEA plastic protection bag n.d.

IKEA (Sweden, est. 1943)
Plastic, 17 x 30" (43.2 x 76.2 cm)

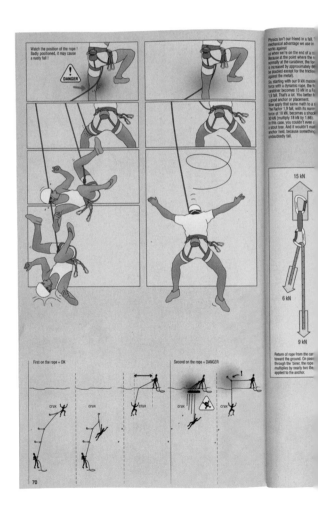

Petzl catalogue of climbing equipment 1997

Petzl International (France, est. 1975)
Paper, 6 ¾ x 11 ¾" (17.1 x 29.8 cm)
Publisher: Petzl International, France (1997)

WARNING
TOBACCO USE CAN MAKE YOU IMPOTENT

Cigarettes may cause sexual impotence due to decreased blood flow to the penis. This can prevent you from having an erection.

Health Canada

Go Smoke Free! Health warning labels for tobacco product packaging 2000

Health Canada, Tobacco Control Programme, Government of Canada

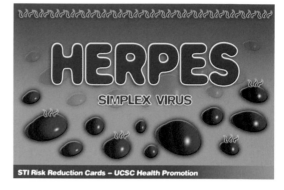

Protect Your Hearing

YOU ARE AT RISK OF HEARING LOSS!

- Hearing damage can take the form of temporary or permanent ringing in the ears (tinnitus) and loss of the ability to hear clearly.
- Amplified music can cause noise-induced hearing loss (NIHL). A study in Great Britain found that 62% of regular clubbers have symptoms of hearing loss.
- The risk of hearing damage depends on: (1) how loud the music is; (2) how close you are to the speakers; (3) how long you are on the dance floor; (4) previous hearing damage.
- You may be at risk if you have a family history of hearing loss.

DO YOU HAVE HEARING DAMAGE?

- You hear ringing in your ears; you're sensitive to loud noises.
- You have difficulty hearing others when there is background noise.
- People sound like they're mumbling or talking too quickly; you have to ask them to repeat themselves.
- You need to turn the volume on the TV or radio higher than others.
- You hear the telephone better through one ear than the other.

If you have any of these symptoms, get your hearing checked by a hearing health professional. To prevent more damage, wear earplugs!

BE AWARE OF YOUR ENVIRONMENT

- Sound levels in dance clubs can be as high as 115 decibels, which can cause damage within a few seconds.

www.justicedesign.com

- Stay at least 10 feet away from the speakers—dancing in front of speakers is very risky.
- Use ear plugs—cotton and rolled up tissue paper provide NO protection.
- Ask that sound levels be turned down if too loud.
- Don't talk on the dance floor—shouting into ears can damage hearing.
- Alcohol and drugs lower your sense of pain and increase the risk of hearing damage. Being tired, dehydrated, or overheated also increase risk.
- Drink plenty of water. Take 10-30 minute breaks where sound levels are lower.
- If you dance a lot or work in a club, consider getting custom earplugs for music attenuation to protect your hearing without distorting sound.

HOW TO USE EARPLUGS

1. With clean hands, roll the earplug until it is as thin as possible.
2. Quickly insert the tapered end all the way into your ear.
3. Hold it in place for at least 30 seconds until it fully expands.
4. Release the earplug then gently push it in one more time to ensure a complete fit. The end should be even with the opening of your ear canal.

DANCESAFE.
Promoting Health and Safety within the Rave and Nightclub Community

www.dancesafe.org

HERPES SIMPLEX VIRUS

HERPES SIMPLEX VIRUS

UCSC Health Promotion
831.459.3772 : hpromo@ucsc.edu

WHAT IS IT?

Herpes is a sexually transmitted infection (STI) caused by the herpes simplex viruses type 1 (HSV-1) and type 2 (HSV-2). Type 1 is commonly known as "oral herpes" and type 2 as "genital herpes." However, both can infect the genitals. It is estimated that 1 in 4 adults has genital herpes caused by either HSV-1 or HSV-2.

HOW IS IT TRANSMITTED?

Herpes is most commonly transmitted via sores caused by the virus. However, it is possible to become infected when no sores are visibly present on the genitals or mouth. A person can get oral herpes (HSV-1) by coming into contact with the saliva of an infected person. Oral herpes (HSV-1) can also infect the genitals. It is therefore possible to contract oral herpes on either the mouth or genitals (HSV-1) through oral-genital contact. Genital herpes (HSV-2) is transmitted through genital-genital contact. In rare cases genital herpes (HSV-2) can be transmitted to the mouth.

WHAT ARE THE SYMPTOMS?

Herpes symptoms range from no visible signs to painful blisters. Other symptoms include red/itchy/tingling areas, red bumps, or tiny scratches. For males, this can occur on the penis, pubic area, buttocks, and/or scrotum. For females, this can occur on the outer vaginal lips, buttocks or pubic area.

www.justicedesign.com

HOW IS IT DIAGNOSED?

During an examination a swab can be taken of the infected area when symptoms are present. A blood test can also be done if someone is asymptomatic.

HOW IS IT TREATED?

There is no treatment that will cure herpes. However, antiviral medications can shorten and prevent outbreaks while a person takes the medication.

WANNA KNOW MORE?

Check out these resources for more information!

www.plannedparenthood.org
www.familydoctor.org
www.medlineplus.gov
www.cdc.gov
www2.ucsc.edu/healthcenter
www.ashastd.org/hrc

CDC National STD/AIDS Hotline: (800) 227-8922 or (800) 342-2437
National Herpes Hotline: (919) 361-8488

All statistics are from the CDC
If you have further questions please consult a clinician

UCSC Health Promotion

DanceSafe Protect Your Hearing Harm Reduction Card (above) 2005

Sexually Transmitted Infection (STI) Risk Reduction Cards (above right and opposite) 2004

Jason Justice (American, born 1973)
JusticeDesign (USA, est. 2000)
6 x 4" (15.2 x 10.2 cm)

(above) Manufacturer: DanceSafe, USA (2005)

(above right and opposite) Manufacturer: University of California Santa Cruz Health Promotion, USA (2004)

STI Risk Reduction Cards – UCSC Health Promotion

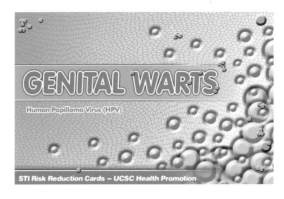

Human Papilloma Virus (HPV)

STI Risk Reduction Cards – UCSC Health Promotion

GONORRHEA

UCSC Health Promotion
831.459.3772 : hpromo@ucsc.edu

WHAT IS IT?
Gonorrhea is caused by the bacterium *Neisseria gonorrhoeae*. It grows in warm, moist areas of the female reproductive tract including the cervix (opening to the womb), uterus (womb), and fallopian tubes (egg canals). The bacteria can also grow in the mouth, throat, urethra, and anus of both males and females. 650,000 people are diagnosed with gonorrhea each year in the U.S. and 75% are 15-29 years old.

HOW IS IT TRANSMITTED?
Gonorrhea can be transmitted whether or not the infected person shows any symptoms. It can be spread through direct vaginal, anal and/or oral contact. Ejaculation does not need to occur for it to be transmitted. Because direct contact with an infected area is necessary for transmission, gonorrhea cannot be spread through objects such as towels or toilet seats.

WHAT ARE THE SYMPTOMS?
10% of males and 20-40% of females are symptom free. If present, symptoms usually appear within 2-5 days of infection.

FEMALES:
• Burning/pain during urination
• Yellow or bloody vaginal discharge
• Pelvic pain

MALES:
• Burning sensation during urination
• Yellow-white discharge from the penis
• Painful or swollen testicles

HOW IS IT DIAGNOSED?
Testing for gonorrhea involves an examination, during which fluid samples are taken from any areas exposed to infection. Urine testing is also available.

HOW IS IT TREATED?
Gonorrhea is usually treated with an antibiotic prescribed by a doctor.

WANNA KNOW MORE?
Check out these resources for more information!

www.plannedparenthood.org
www.familydoctor.org
www.medlineplus.gov
www.cdc.gov
www2.ucsc.edu/healthcenter

CDC National STD/AIDS Hotline: (800) 227-8922 or (800) 342-2437
National Herpes Hotline: (919) 361-8488

All statistics are from the CDC
If you have further questions please consult a clinician

UCSC Health Promotion

GENITAL WARTS (HPV)

UCSC Health Promotion
831.459.3772 : hpromo@ucsc.edu

WHAT IS IT?
Genital HPV is a sexually transmitted infection (STI) effecting the genital area. HPV is the name of a group of viruses that includes more than 100 different strains. The effects of these strains vary and include mild pap smear abnormalities, genital warts, and cancer of the cervix, anus and penis.

HOW IS IT TRANSMITTED?
HPV is transmitted through skin-to-skin genital contact with an infected partner. The virus can be transmitted without visible warts being present. HPV is NOT transmitted through blood or genital secretions. 50-75% of sexually active males and females acquire a genital HPV infection, with 5.5 million Americans acquire a new genital HPV infection each year.

WHAT ARE THE SYMPTOMS?
Most people with a genital HPV infection have no signs or symptoms. Other people get visible genital warts. Genital warts are growths or bumps that form a cauliflower-like shape.

HOW IS IT DIAGNOSED?
Most females are diagnosed with HPV on the basis of abnormal Pap smears. Tests are available for males as well.

HOW IS IT TREATED?
There is no "cure" for HPV, although most infections appear temporary and are probably cleared by the body's immune system. Cancer-related types are more likely to persist and can lead to cervical, penile and anal cancer. Genital warts can be treated and cured with a topical cream or liquid nitrogen freezing.

WANNA KNOW MORE?
Check out these resources for more information!

www.plannedparenthood.org
www.familydoctor.org
www.medlineplus.gov
www.cdc.gov
www2.ucsc.edu/healthcenter

CDC National STD/AIDS Hotline: (800) 227-8922 or (800) 342-2437
National HPV Hotline: (919) 361-4848

All statistics are from the CDC
If you have further questions please consult a clinician

UCSC Health Promotion

DanceSafe is a nonprofit organization whose goal is to promote health and safety in nightclubs and raves—large, often unregulated dance parties held in the most diverse venues. California-based graphic designer Jason Justice has designed a series of cards for DanceSafe to provide information on some necessary preoccupations for the electronic dance community, such as driving home safely and protecting one's hearing from loud music. Justice has also developed a series of Sexually Transmitted Infection (STI) Risk Reduction Cards for the University of California Santa Cruz Health Promotion, in which he juxtaposes colorful eye-catching graphics with serious health and safety information about the corresponding STI.

The aim of these seductive graphics is to reach a young audience and deliver a clear and incisive message, thus furthering awareness and safety.

—R. L.

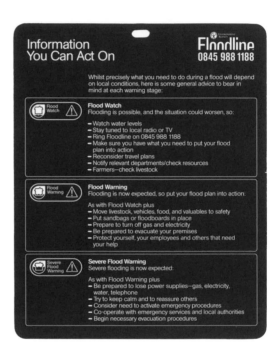

**Guide to the
Flood Warning Codes** 1999

North Design (UK, est. 1995)
Polypropylene, 7 ¼ x 9" (18.3 x 22.8 cm)
Manufacturer: Environment Agency, UK (2000)

Argus3 Thermal Imaging Camera 2002

James Lamb (British, born 1971)
Alloy Ltd. Total Product Design (UK, est. 1999)
Radel 5100 thermoplastic and Santoprene elastomer,
11 3/4 x 7 1/8 x 10 5/8" (30 x 18 x 27 cm)
Manufacturer: e2v Technologies, Ltd., UK (2002),
licensed by Argus Industries, Inc.

Baby Zoo Rug and **Good Night
Night Light** 2003

Laurene Leon Boym (American, born 1964)
Boym Partners, Inc. (USA, est. 1986)
Wool, polycarbonate, and LED's, carpet: 59 x 39⅜"
(150 x 100 cm); light: 1¼ x 7⅛" (3.3 x 18 cm) diam.
Manufacturer: Flos S.p.A., Italy (2003)

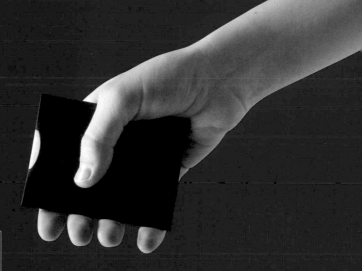

Flashcard 1993

Iain Sinclair (British, born 1943)
Cardboard and incandescent light bulbs,
3 ¼ x 2 ¾ x ⁹⁄₁₆" (8.4 x 7 x 0.5 cm)
Manufacturer: Torchco Ltd., UK (1997)

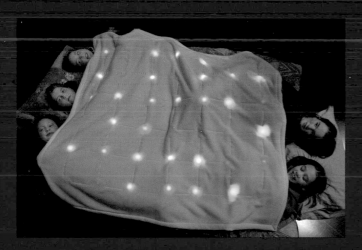

Light Blanket Prototype. 2002

James McAdam (British, born 1977)
Electronic components and fabric,
59 x 59" (150 x 150 cm)

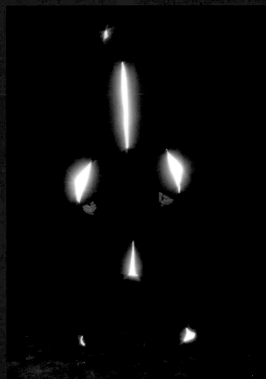

See and Be Seen (SABS) Parka 2001

Adam Thorpe (Welsh, born 1969) and **Joe Hunter**
(British, born 1967) of **Vexed Generation** (UK, est. 1994)
Corwool, Teflon, and 3M Scotchlite Reflective Material
Manufacturer: Vexed Generation Clothing, Ltd., UK (2001)

Teeth Dot Alert Prototype. 2001

Martí Guixé (Spanish, born 1964)
Reflective vinyl, ¼" (0.5 cm) diam.

Hot Box Prototype. 2003

Ana Mir (Spanish, born 1969) and
Emili Padrós (Spanish, born 1969) of
emiliana design studio (Spain, est. 1996)
Polyethylene, 7 x 23 ⅝ x 15 ¾" (18 x 60 x 40 cm)

Hot Box is a translucent pedestal that emerges from the ground, radiates heat, and emits light, offering comfort and visibility and thus protection for those who spend long periods of time in the street, for instance, sex workers. When not in use, Hot Box remains flat and integrated and hidden in the pavement. The project was part of the *Urban Therapies* exhibition at the Col.legi d'Arquitectes de Catalunya in 2003, organized by Ana Mir. The show presented projects and installations by young designers, as part of the series *<40 (under 40)*. Their designs were envisioned as "therapeutical interventions" and a reflection on some of the situations in public spaces in Barcelona, from transportation to prostitution. The Hot Box could be installed at several points throughout the city, creating a new urban landscape.

For background on the emiliana design studio, see page 91.   —P. J.

Camcopter S-100
Unmanned Aerial Vehicle 2004

Gerhard Heufler (Austrian, born 1944)
Carbon-fiber and titanium, 41" x 49" x 10' 1⁵⁄₈"
(104.2 x 123.8 x 310 cm)
Manufacturer: Schiebel Elektronische Geraete GmbH,
Austria (2005)

The Vienna-based company Schiebel is one of the leaders in the field of mine-detection equipment, specializing in humanitarian de-mining since the 1970s. As part of the UAV (Unmanned Aerial Vehicle) program, the original Camcopter 5.1 had been in service since 1999.

Schiebel has just developed the next generation, the Camcopter S-100, a compact and light-weight helicopter with an autonomous flight-control system. Besides transmitting its position and receiving control inputs from a control station in real time, an onboard navigation computer ensures continuous operation independent of the command post. A fixed-mounted daylight camera provides the operator with situational awareness and flight orientation. In addition to the onboard generator, a back-up battery guarantees power supply in emergencies.

Although the Camcopter was originally designed for aerial mine detection, it has proved its efficiency in a number of other applications: border and harbor patrol; antismuggling actions; tactical surveillance, including maritime reconnaissance; fire-fighting in forests; monitoring natural disasters; flood relief; search and rescue of missing persons in inaccessible areas; surveillance of oil pipelines, railways, industrial plants, water, power, and communication lines; precise dropping of humanitarian aid in nonaccessible areas; cartographic studies and surveys; scientific measurements; and pest control in agriculture. A universal payload mount can be fitted with a wide variety of data, which facilitates a flexible and rapid response to changing mission requirements. —P. J.

SPLICE low-cost
land-mine detector Prototype. 1997

Chris Richardson (British, born 1941)
Aluminum and fiberglass, head: 7 $\frac{7}{8}$ x 5 $\frac{7}{8}$"
(20 x 15 cm); length: 49 $\frac{1}{4}$" (125 cm)
Prototype by Roke Manor Research, Ltd.,
a Siemens company, UK (1999)

Every twenty minutes someone somewhere is killed or mutilated by a land mine. These weapons remain in the ground long after the conflict ends. No one knows exactly how many mines lie in the soil; estimates range from sixty to a hundred million, in countries that have been the scene of past conflicts like Angola, Somalia, Afghanistan, Mozambique, Cambodia, Bosnia, Croatia, and Kosovo. Each year about twenty-five thousand people take that fatal step. Apart from the human cost, mines also destabilize the economic prospect of the land in which they lie. They have a paralyzing effect, contaminating fertile fields, cutting off access to markets, schools, and water supplies, holding people hostage in their own villages, or displacing them from their homes.

Compared to the astonishing number of land mines in war-torn countries, only about one hundred thousand are cleared every year, mostly because of the high cost of detection and clearance equipment, maintenance, and trained operators. It costs only about three dollars to build a mine and as little as one minute and negligible skills to plant it, while it could cost up to one thousand dollars to detect and destroy a single mine. Far more mines could be cleared each year if the cost of de-mining was substantially reduced.

The SPLICE—Self Powered Locator and Identifier for Concealed Equipment—is a simple land-mine detector that can be produced for twenty-five dollars, a more reasonable price for developing countries. The self-powered detector requires no batteries; the regular side to side motion of the device by the de-miner is enough to activate the generator. The emission of radio frequencies identifies any sort of anomaly on the ground, thus pointing to the location of plastic and metal objects, which an operator can distinguish by listening to tonal differences through headphones. When the device detects a mine, it emits an audible signal like a steady clicking. Considering the recent, and already banned, introduction of the plastic mine, this feature turns out to be key.

The creator of the SPLICE, Chris Richardson, explains how they "wanted to devise a cheap machine that could be issued to everyone in a village." The designer states that if mass-produced, his low-cost mine detector could halve the rate of mine casualties.   —P. J.

MIMID Mini Mine Detector 1996

Gerhard Heufler (Austrian, born 1944)
Carbon fiber, 12 ⁷⁄₈ x 4 x 2 ¹⁄₄" (32.8 x 10.2 x 5.6 cm)
folded; 49 ³⁄₄" (126.2 cm) extended
Manufacturer: Schiebel Elektronische Geraete GmbH,
Austria (2005)

Heufler Design's MIMID has been used for minimal metal mine detection in both military and humanitarian operations for almost ten years. The one-piece, lightweight, compact, and collapsible design makes it suitable for remote areas with limited logistical support. When folded, the unit can be carried on a waist belt or in a pocket, and can be set up in less than thirty seconds. The de-miner can adjust the telescopic shaft sections to operate in a standing, kneeling, or prone position. The six-pound device, which is four feet in length when unfolded, is powered by four AA batteries located in the handle. The electronic controls are also concentrated in a single unit within easy reach of the user. The collapsible frame and the unique hollow-rectangular shape of the search head make it particularly suitable for confined places and for areas with heavy vegetation, and it can even be used under water.

Operator training requires only a few minutes, which makes it a valuable asset, almost like a first-aid kit, especially for humanitarian organizations. The MIMID, conceived to be easily operated by both specialists and occasional volunteers, provides them with the immediate means of enhancing safety in countries where mines are a constant threat.

—P. J.

Spider Boot Antipersonnel Mine
Foot Protection System 1998

Gad Shaanan Design, Inc. (USA, est. 1981)
Thermoplastics and proprietary composites,
20 ½ x 8 ⅝ x 13" (52 x 22 x 33 cm)
Manufacturer: Med-Eng Systems, Inc., Canada (2005)

The Spider boot, shown here as part of a complete de-mining equipment unit, is built on a platform that is 5 ¾ inches (14.4 centimeters) off the ground, providing a standoff distance from a detonating mine while keeping feet and legs as far away as possible from the explosion. The boot also incorporates self-sacrificing materials, such as aluminum honeycomb encased in a V-shaped steel container on the underside of the platform to absorb the impact of the detonation. The raised platform provides for an area to deflect shrapnel, reducing the number of land-mine-related amputations.

De-mining devices and sniffing dogs now have some competition in the detection of land mines: the Belgian company APOPO has trained African giant pouch rats, while researchers at the University of Montana have been using honeybees to screen large areas. The Danish company Aresa Biodetection has developed genetically engineered plants sensitive to nitrogen dioxide that change color from green to red when in contact with contaminated soil.

Although the 1997 international treaty to ban land mines, known as the Ottawa Treaty, was enforced in 1999, more than forty countries still refuse to sign it, including Russia, China, India, and the U.S. Several nongovernmental organizations and mine-awareness and victim-assistance programs like HALO Trust (Hazardous Areas Life-Support Organization), Stop Mines, International Campaign to Ban Landmines, Landmine Survivors Network, and Humanitarian Demining, keep working to disarm these weapons, allowing the affected communities to return to their homelands without fear. —R. L. & P. J.

The planning of *SAFE* began in March 2001, and a diverse team of colleagues, volunteers, friends, and accidental consultants contributed immeasurably to its realization. Many people have expended enormous time and energy to help bring this exhibition to fruition, and I will be forever indebted to them. On behalf of The Museum of Modern Art, I wish to thank the designers and manufacturers featured in the exhibition, catalogue, and website for their cooperation, enthusiasm, and generosity. I also wish to thank the sponsors for making this endeavor possible, and the lenders for agreeing to part, temporarily, with their possessions.

acknowledgments

In the research phase, I relied on two exceptional design minds, architect Gregg Pasquarelli and designer Hella Jongerius, who, with me, organized the 2003 International Design Conference in Aspen, Colorado, devoted to the subject of design and safety. My gratitude also goes to all the participants in the conference, and a few in particular: Susan Yelavich and Cameron Sinclair, Ezri Tarazi and Marc Sadler, and James Sanders, Bill Joy, David Levy, Stefan Sagmeister, and Bruce Schneier.

A number of advisers and sources gave us useful information and insights. We would like to thank Stephanie Davies, Guillaume le Duc, Christopher Sauer, William Conk, and Sula Al Naqeeb at Doctors Without Borders; Jennifer Clark, Yusus Hassan, and Joung-Ah Ghedini at UNHCR; Sandie Blanchet at UNICEF; Llenay Ferretti from Ten Thousand Villages; Robin McCune from the American Heart Association; Nancy A. Cowles from Kids in Danger; Mark Conroy from the National Fire Protection Association; the New York Fire Department; Jeffrey Escoffier and Kesu James at the City of New York Department of Health and Mental Hygiene; Peter Lochery from CARE and the Millennium Water Alliance; Nigel Robinson from HALO; Karen Welter at the Landmine Survivors Network; Jodi Williams at the International Campaign to Ban Landmines; the United Nations Mine Action Service; and Lukas Einsele with his *One Step Beyond* project on de-mining.

Many friends and colleagues sent ideas and objects for consideration and gave precious advice and assistance. I would like to thank them all, but space limitations make this impossible. However, I must single out the following: Kelley Beaverford, Kathy Benardo, Georg Bertsch, Guus Beumer, George Beylerian, Andrew Bolton, Michael Bzdak, Miguel Calvo, Emily Campbell, Michele Caniato, Arthur Ceria, Clara Cervera, Medardo Chiapponi, Allan Chochinov, Ofer Cohen, William Conk, Björn Dahlström, Alon Daniel, Andrew Dent, Tom Dixon, Eva Dringel-Techt, Yoshiko Ebihara, Li Edelkoort, Rafi Elbaz, Michael Erlhoff, Lisa Frigand, Lisa Gabor, Leslie Gill, Dorothy Globus, Kristina Goodrich, Carma Goran, Chantal Hamaïde, Claire Hartten, Kim Hastreiter, Steven Heller, Sarah Herda, Kigge Hvid, Hiroshi Ishii, John Jay, Hiroko Kasai, David Kelley, Robert Kloos, Seungyoon Lee, Ellen Lupton, Paul Makovsky, Fern Mallis, Jennifer Mano, Carlo McCormick, Alessia Melchiori, Ana Mir, Christian Moeller, Marie Moreira, Whitney Mortimer, Cary Murnion, Nobi Nakanishi, Jane Nisselson, Lucy Orta, Dorthe Paulsen, Sean Perkins, Allen Prusis, Vivek Radhakrishnan,

Alice Rawsthorn, Julie Schlosser, Paul Sullivan, Ilkka Suppanen, Andras Szanto, Gigi Thomson, Henry Urbach, Gary van Deursen, Luis Villegas, Peter Wheelwright, Jason Winocour, Laetitia Wolff, and Aska Yokoyama. I also wish to thank the following professors and design schools: Tom Barker at the Royal College of Art, Elle-Mie Ejdrup Hansen at Designskolen Kolding, Lorraine Gamman at Central Saint Martins College of Art and Design, and Pierre Keller and Alexis Georgacopoulos at the École cantonale d'art de Lausanne; as well as the students from my seminar at the Harvard University Graduate School of Design in spring of 2005: Shannon Loew, T.A., and Rajib Adikhary, Michi Akutsu, Marit Dewhurst, Matthew Fajkus, James Hollingsworth, Jr., Catherine Sam Johnston, Ira Jones, Nicole Keith, Raina Kumra, Robert Langley, Fotini Lazaridou-Hatzigoga, Hui-Ting Lin, Julia Ogrydziak, Yekta Pakdaman-Hamedani, Salma Ting, and Martin Wellnitz. A very special mention goes to Larry Carty, who has shared every single doubt, detail, discovery, and development of the show and whose enthusiasm for my ideas has never wavered.

The staff at The Museum of Modern Art deserves special acknowledgment for their passionate support. In particular, I wish to thank Agnes Gund, President Emerita, and Ronald Lauder, Chairman Emeritus of the Board, knowledgeable and enthusiastic fans of design; Marie-Josée Kravis, President, and Robert Menschel, Chairman of the Board, for their unrelenting trust in the Museum's curators; Glenn D. Lowry, Director, whose early and unwavering support was crucial to the realization of the exhibition; and Jennifer Russell, Senior Deputy Director of Exhibitions, Collections, and Programs, for successfully bringing this huge ship to port. I also thank Maria DeMarco Beardsley, Coordinator of Exhibitions, and Carlos Yepes, Associate Coordinator, for working out the complicated administrative details; Jennifer Wolfe, Senior Assistant Registrar, Kerry McGinnity, Senior Registrar Assistant, and Ellen Conti, Registrar Assistant, for keeping track of the diverse loan items; Kim Mitchell, Director of Communications, Daniela Stigh, Manager of Communications, and Matthew Montgomery, Senior Publicist, for taking good care of the press and building up great expectations; Michael Margitich, Deputy Director, External Affairs, Todd Bishop, Director, Exhibition Funding, and Mary Hannah, Assistant Director, for their efforts in securing funding for the show; and Peter Foley, Director of Marketing, and Mark Swartz, Editor/Writer, for marketing it. I also wish to thank Stephen Clark, Deputy General Counsel, and Nancy Adelson, Associate General Counsel, for their invaluable advice; and in the Department of Education, David Little, Director, Adult and Academic Programs, and Laura Beiles and Sara Bodinson, Assistant Educators, for their great work organizing the public programs and coordinating the Acoustiguido tour, respectively. I would also like to extend thanks to Roger Griffith, Associate Sculpture Conservator; Rob Jung, Assistant Manager and Location Manager; Elizabeth Riggle and Scott Hook, Preparators; Lauren Solotoff, Assistant Director of Merchandising; Bonnie Mackay, Director of Creative, Marketing, and Merchandising for MoMA Retail, and the rest of their team in the Retail Department: Chay Costello, Jennifer Hom, Seokhee Lee, and Dawn Bossman; Eliza Sparacino, Manager, and

Gael Lelamer, Senior CEMS Assistant, Collection and Exhibition Technologies; and Jennifer Tobias, Librarian, Reference and Acquisitions, for her enthusiastic assistance on our research.

A special acknowledgment and my gratitude go to the Department of Publications, in particular to Christina Grillo, Associate Production Manager, who solved all problems and kept everyone on schedule, and Joanne Greenspun, Senior Editor, for her guidance and supervision of the editorial process. Many thanks also to Amanda Washburn, Senior Book Designer, who designed the catalogue beautifully and also quickly. Thanks also to Tom Griesel, Collections Photographer, and James Kuo, Senior Designer in the Department of Graphic Design, for their photographs of some of the objects included in the catalogue. Bonnie Ralston, Senior Designer in the Department of Graphic Design, is responsible for the graphics throughout the exhibition and its installation.

The installation was indeed a challenge even for our heroic Department of Exhibition Design and Production, directed by Jerome Neuner. David Hollely, Production Manager, designed the installation with his incomparable crew, and K Mita, Associate Director of Information Technology, along with his whole team, performed miracles in order to ensure that the technology worked smoothly and effectively.

For the *SAFE* website, designed by OrdinaryKids, my thanks go to Allegra Burnette, Creative Manager of Digital Media, and Shannon Darrough, Associate Producer, who together with the designers were precious interlocutors and an inexhaustible source of new ideas. Alexandra Quantrill, an intern in our curatorial department, produced most of the materials on the website.

In the Department of Architecture and Design, I am deeply grateful to Terence Riley, the Philip Johnson Chief Curator of Architecture and Design, who believed strongly in this exhibition and offered his support throughout the project. The entire department was encouraging and helpful, and I thank each of its members, especially Rachel Judlowe, Coordinator, and Curbie Oestreich, Manager. A special mention also goes to Candace Banks for her precious assistance. Several brilliant interns worked on this project. I wish to thank Christine Canabou, David Fierman, Rachael Lindhagen, Julia Neira, Daniela Sloninsky, and Susan Walsh. Special thanks also go to Hideki Yamamoto, who helped us secure many loans in Asia and contributed ideas, texts, and invaluable criticism.

Lastly, I would like to thank the person with whom I shared all the adventure, Patricia Juncosa Vecchierini. Her title is Curatorial Assistant, but she has been much more than that. The pillar on which the whole construction has rested, she has been unbelievably patient, always keeping everything in perspective and never forgetting the details that make all the difference. She has proven to be an incomparable collaborator.

In conclusion, I would like to mention Todd Haynes's 1995 movie *Safe*, whose contents, especially the opening titles designed by the New York-based company Bureau, have inspired the title of this show.

Paola Antonelli
Curator, Department of Architecture and Design

index of illustrations

a

von den Acker, Laurens: Glo Car, 32

Adachi Shiki Kogyo Co., Ltd., Japan, 154, 170

Adler, Deborah: Target ClearRx prescription system, 182

Aguilar, Javier Senosiain: Shark House, 19

Air France Passenger Briefing Cards, 189

Akai, Yoko: Fresh Kiss Breath Checker, 146

Aliph, USA, 136

Alloy, Ltd., Total Product Design, UK, 195

American Red Cross Oregon Trail Chapter, USA: Prepare Oregon UNDERtheTABLE Workstation Safety Kit, 150

Amishay, Yair: Shimonit Head Guard, 167

Anastassiades, Michael: Hide Away Furniture, 72; Priscila Huggable Atomic Mushroom, 8

A-net, Inc., Japan, 70

Antenna Design, USA, 116, 187

Apothecary Products, Inc., USA, 181

Architecture and Vision, Germany, 64

Arif, Omri: Shimonit Head Guard, 167

Armellino, Stephen: Bullet-Resistant Mask, 81

Asikainen, Teppo: Swell Soundwave Panels, 137

Augustin, Stephan: Watercone, 140

AutoSock AS, Norway, 170

b

Ban, Shigeru: Paper Log House–Turkey, 61

Bård Eker Industrial Design, Norway, 126

Barnes, Richard: *Icturus Galbula Parvus (Northern Oriole*, 16; Underground shelter at Greenbriar Hotel, 23

BBP Arkitekter, Denmark, 177

Becker, Pierre: FreeCharge Mobile Phone Charger, 172

Beedholm, Mikkel: Design for a Mobile HIV/AIDS Health Clinic, 46

Béhar, Yves: Aliph Jawbone Headset, 136; Tylenol Bottle Concept, 131

Beige Design, USA, 161

Bernardo Gutiérrez and Ana Martínez, Mexico, 176

Bezalel Research & Development, Bezalel Academy of Art and Design: Bardas Protection System for Adults, 168; Bardas Protection System for Children, 168; Mini Mamat Babies Protection System for Babies, 168; Shmartaf Protection System for Toddlers, 168

Biomega, Denmark: Puma Bike, 103

Blanc, Sighild: Crazypack Cigarette Package Covers, 134

Blingks, Sweden, 114

Blizzard Protection Systems, Ltd., UK, 157

Bloomberg L.P., USA, 116

de Boer, Rob: Mojo Barrier, 94

Bone, Brian: Solo Traveler Plus re-closable hot cup lid, 144

Borland, Ralph: Suited for Subversion, 84

Boym, Laurene Leon: Baby Zoo Rug, 196; Good Night Night Light, 196

Boym Partners, Inc., USA, 196

Bravis International, Ltd., Japan, 132

Bregenhøj, Torben: Life-Saving Station, 177

van den Bremen, Cindy: Capsters Sports Headgear for Muslim Women, Tennis, Aerobics, and Outdoors versions, 138

Breuker, Margaret: BananaBunker, 133

Brookdale International Systems, Inc., Canada, 165

Brunton, USA, 172

Brunton company design, USA: Solar Roll 14 Flexible Solar Panel, 172

Bruun, Poul Allan: How to Disappear kit and vending machine, 78

Buchenau, Marion: As Time Goes By card, 115

Burns, Bill: Safety Gear for Small Animals, 158

c

Callan, Matthew: Lifeline AED Semiautomatic External Defibrillator, 152

Capsters, The Netherlands, 138

Cárdenas Osuna, Raúl: Securitree, 176

Carius, Marcus: EVAC+ Emergency Escape Smoke Hood, 165

Carl Mertens, Germany: Oyster Glove chain mail glove, 88 (see also Mertens, Carl)

Carlson, Dennis: Emergency Safety Kit, 171

208

Carlson Technology, Inc., USA, **171**

Chapman, Dean: Personal SafetyVest, **164**

Charbonnel, Mickaël: PowerPizza, **106**

Chatillon, Frédéric: Crazypack Cigarette Package Covers, **134**

Chen, Karen: MultiCam Multi-Environment Camouflage, **77**

Chi, Benny: Lifeline AED Semiautomatic External Defibrillator, **152**

Clean Call, USA, **135**

Cobigo, Stéphanie: SBC SC605 In-Touch Address Recorder, **186**

Cohen, Michal: Shimonit Head Guard, **167**

Coloplast: Band-Aid Advanced Healing Blister, **128**

Coloplast A/S, Denmark, **129**

Colwell, Rita: Safe Sari, **141**

Computer Design, Inc., USA, **164**

Conduit Group, USA, **85**

Con Edison, Inc., **95**

C.P. Company, Italy, **66**

crasset, matali: No TV Today and No PC Today, TV and PC parasites, **71**; Polygloo baby carrier, **121**

Creswell Manufacturing, India, **95**

Crye Associates, USA, **77**

Crye, Caleb: MultiCam Multi-Environment Camouflage, **77**

Crye Precision, USA, **77**

Cultured Containers, USA, **133**

d

van Dam, Hein: Guardian Angel handbag, **113**

DanceSafe, USA, **192**

Dave Porter and Jackie Demchuk, Canada, **158**

Debika Corporation, Japan, **164**

Debika Planning Room, Japan: High-Grade Protective Hood for Emergency, **164**

Defibtech, LLC, USA, **152**

Design against Crime Research Initiative, Central Saint Martins College of Art and Design, UK, **104–09**

Design Continuum Seoul, Korea, **187**

Designskolen Kolding, Denmark, **78**, **162**

De Wisselstroom, The Netherlands, **74**

Dolan, Monina Johnson: Courtesy Blood Card, **115**

Dolmen, G&A, prnc, France, **134**

Doty, Heath; Solo Traveler Plus re-closable hot cup lid, **144**

Drach, Ami: Hamsa Head Guard, **167**

Dräger Safety AG & Co., Germany, **153**

DuCast, United Arab Emirates, **95**

Dunne, Anthony: Electro-draught Excluder, **72**; Faraday Chair, **73**; Hide Away Furniture, **72**, Priscila l luggable Atomic Mushroom, **8**

Dyrvang, Luca Leo Funch: How to Disappear kit and vending machine, **78**

e

ECCLES, China, **95**

e2v Technologies, Ltd., UK, **195**

École cantonale d'art de Lausanne (ECAL), Switzerland, **160**

Edra S.p.A., Italy, **127**

Egnor, Virginia Ruth ("Dagmar"), **29**

Eisenman, Peter: House VI Fourteen Transformations, **22**

Electroland, USA, **67**

Elkstrand, Glenn: Lumber pro

class 3 Safety Boot, **90**

emiliana design studio, Spain, **90**, **199**

Endo, Suzue: Otohime YES300D artificial sound machine for the bathroom, **76**

Eng, Gin L.: Con Edison Cast Iron Covers, Type Q-8-VI, for Electric Manholes, **95**

Environment Agency, UK, **194**

d'Esposito, Martino: Swiss Fondue Earthquake Safety Table, **160**

EVAC+ Design/Engineering Team, Canada, **165**

f

Fagum-Stomil S.A., Poland, **90**

Faulders, Thom: Undercover Table, **161**

Fehlberg, Eric: MultiCam Multi-Environment Camouflage, **77**

Ferrara, Daniel: Global Village Shelter, **60**

Ferrara Design, Inc., USA, **60**

Ferrara, Mia: Global Village Shelter, **60**

Ferrari, Moreno: Parka/Air Mattress, **66**

Fischer, Kurt: HeartStart Onsite Defibrillator, **152**

Flos S.p.A., Italy, **196**

Ford Motor Company: Glo Car, **32**

Franceschini, Amy: Homeland Security Blanket, **71**

Frandsen, Mikkel Vestergaard: PermaNet 2.0 Long-Lasting Insecticidal Mosquito Net, **62**; Zerofly Plastic Sheeting with Incorporated Insecticide, **62**

Frandsen, Torben Vestergaard: PermaNet 2.0 Long-Lasting Insecticidal Mosquito Net, **62**; Zerofly Plastic Sheeting with Incorporated Insecticide, **62**

Frederiksen, Michael: Sea Shelter, **162**

Freeplay Energy plc, South Africa, **173**

Freeplay Energy plc, South Africa, and Motorola, Inc., USA, **172**

Freeplay Foundation and Freeplay Energy plc: Lifeline radio, **11**

French, Ronald J.: Lifestat Emergency Pocket Airway, **150**

Frostholm, Christian Yde: Vigilance Propreté, **14**

Fryatt, Tim: NoGo Barrier New York Financial District Streetscape and Security Design, **97**

Fukasawa, Naoto: Sole Bag, **124**

fuseproject, USA, **131**, **136**

Futurefarmers, USA, **171**

g

Gad Shaanan Design, Inc, USA: Spider Boot Antipersonnel Mine Foot Protection System, **203**

Galante, Maurizio: Bullet-resistant blouson, **87**; Killing Zones shirt, **86**; T-shirt and vest, **86**

Gamman, Lorraine: "Keep Your Bag Safe!" Flyer, **106**; Stop Thief! Bentwood Chair Clone, **105**; Stop Thief! Ply Chair, **104**

Ganchrow, Dov: Hamsa Head Guard, **167**

Garde, Nikhil: Sea Shelter, **162**

General Motors: Cadillac, **29**

Georgia Institute of Technology, USA, **179**

Gerber company design: Infant Spoons, soft bite safety spoons, **125**

Gerber Products Company, USA, **125**

Gerzsenyi, Erika: Personal SafetyVest, **164**

GIANTmicrobes, Inc., USA, **147**

Giro Sport Design, Inc., USA, **81**

Global Village Shelters, LLC, USA, **60**

Grimes, Craig: Ten-element Blood-sugar Monitoring Implant for Diabetics, **178**

Groulx, Ian: Crave Aid satiety patches, **130**

Guillet, Gauthier: Crazypack Cigarette Package Covers, **134**

Guixé, Martí: Teeth Dot Alert, **198**

h

Hanning, Bernard William: 3-in-1 Inflatable Kite/Splint/Body Warmer, **156**

Hansen, Anders: AutoSock, **170**; Startloop car battery starting device, **171**

Hansen, Elle-Mie Ejdrup: Sea Shelter, **162**

Hansen, Eva Jarl: Life-Saving Station, **177**

Hansen, Gunner: Life-Saving Station, **177**

Hansen, Mads Mandrup: Design for a Mobile HIV/AIDS Health Clinic, **46**

Hansen, Morten Just: How to Disappear kit and vending machine, **78**

Hardy, Scott: Industrial Overshoe/TPU 12, **90**

Hareide Designmill, Norway, **170**, **171**

Hareide, Einar: AutoSock, **170**; Startloop car battery starting device, **171**

Health Canada, Tobacco Control Programme, Government of Canada: Go Smoke Free! Health warning labels for tobacco product packaging, **191**

Heath, Stephen: SBC SC605 In-Touch Address Recorder, **186**

Helly Hansen company design, Norway: Oscar Inflatable Life Jacket 150N, **163**

Heufler, Gerhard: Camcopter S-100 Unmanned Aerial Vehicle, **200**; MIMID Mini Mine Detector, **202**

Hiraishi, Kazuhiro: The Corner-Cut Carton, **132**

Hoffmann, Kim: Subtle Safety Defensive Ring, **112**

Human Beans, UK, **106**

Humanscale Safety Products, USA, **164**

Hunter, Joe: Karryfront Screamer bag, **108**; Phonesafe, **109**; Puma Bike, **103**; Scroll Top Backpack, **108**; See and Be Seen (SABS) Parka, **198**

Huq, Anwar: Safe Sari, **141**

Hutchins, Donald: CPR Prompt Rescue Aid, **186**

Hutchinson, John: FreeCharge Mobile Phone Charger, **172**

i

IDEO, USA, **115**, **130**

IDSland, France, **65**, **127**

IKEA, Sweden: IKEA plastic protection bag, **190**

Industrial Design Department, Bezalel Academy of Art and Design, Israel, **82**, **166**, **167**

innovarchi: Gold Coast House, **21**

International Development Enterprises, Bangladesh, **141**

Interware SARL, France, **86**, **87**

Islam, Fakhrul: Shapla Arsenic Removal Filter, **141**

Iwasaki, Ichiro: takata04-neo child car seat, **121**

j

Jansson, Stefan: Safety Concept Car, **26**

Java Jacket, USA, **144**

Jayaraman, Sundaresan: Georgia Tech Wearable Motherboard, **179**

Jex, Inc., Japan, **92**

Johnson & Johnson, USA, **128**

Jönsson A/S, Denmark, **177**

JPMA, France, **151**

JusticeDesign, USA, **192**, **193**

Justice, Jason: DanceSafe Protect Your Hearing Harm Reduction Card, **192**; Sexually Transmitted Infection (STI) Risk Reduction Cards, **192**, **193**

k

K8 Industridesign, Norway, **126**

Kaminski, Vered: Mask Head Guard, **167**

Karrysafe, UK, **108**, **109**

Kevin Biebel, J. Frederick Construction, Inc., USA, **97**

KHR Architects: Design for a Mobile HIV/AIDS Health Clinic, **46**

Kilduff, Ed: Personal SafetyVest, **164**

Kim, Youngmihn: China Telecom Kid Mobile Phone, **187**

Kingsland Color, UK, **106**

Kirin Brewery Co., Ltd., Japan, **132**

Kirps, Paul: protekt, universal protection set, **122**

KNOW HIV/AIDS, **129**

Knox, Amanda: Subtle Safety Defensive Ring, **112**

Koć, Mirazat: Inflate-A-Shield CPR Barrier, **153**

Kolatan/Mac Donald Studio, USA, **99**

Kolatan, Sulan: INVERSAbrane invertible building membrane, **99**

Koller-Craft Manufacturing, Inc., USA, **186**

Koninklijke Begeer BV, The Netherlands, **117**

Koninklijke Philips Electronics N.V., The Netherlands, **186**

Kortschak, Ernest: EVAC+ Emergency Escape Smoke Hood, **165**

Koryo Industrial Co., Ltd., Korea, **142**

Kuroki, Yasuo: Face Guard, **81**

l

Laerdal Medical Corporation Design and Development Team, USA, **153**, **155**

Lamb, James: Argus3 Thermal Imaging Camera, **195**

Lancman, Ial: Bullet-resistant blouson, **87**; Killing Zones shirt, **86**; T-shirt and vest, **86**

Laub, Glenn: Lifeline AED Semiautomatic External Defibrillator, **152**

Lautner, John: Chemosphere, **20**

Ldesign SARL, France, **86**, **87**

Lehanneur, Mathieu: First Mouthful, **184**; Liquid Bone, **185**; Therapeutic Felt-tip Pen, **183**; Therapeutic Handkerchief, **184**; Third Lung, **185**

Levy, Arik: Bullet-resistant blouson, **87**; Killing Zones shirt, **86**; T-shirt and vest, **86**

Leyfert, Jon: Personal SafetyVest, **164**

Liden, Johan: Tylenol Bottle Concept, **131**

Lieu Commun, France, **71**

Local Industries of Güines, Cuba: Raincoat, **139**

Løtveit, Bård: AutoSock, **170**

Lufthansa CityLine Passenger Briefing Cards, **188**

Lyngstadaas, Lars: How to Disappear kit and vending machine, **78**

m

McAdam, James: Light Blanket, **197**; Safe Bedside Table, **113**

McDonald, Bill: INVERSAbrane invertible building membrane, **99**

Machineart, USA, **153**

McKinney, Larry: Inflate-A-Shield CPR Barrier, **153**

McLaren Performance Technologies, Inc., USA, **171**

McNall, Cameron: Urban Nomad Shelter inflatable homeless shelter, **67**

Mc Neill-PPC, Inc., Consumer and Specialty Pharmaceuticals, a Johnson & Johnson company, USA, **131**

Maharishi: Gorscuba jackets, **42**

Mankelow, Jared: Crave Aid satiety patches, **130**

Marbek, UK, **100**

Marcussen, Jan: Compeed X-TREME Flex, **129**

Marion Gillet, Creative Product Development, UK, **106**

Marshall, Mark: FreeCharge Mobile Phone Charger, **172**

Marting, Greg: Giro Atmos bicycle helmet, **81**

Marvel, Jonathan: NoGo Barrier New York Financial District Streetscape and Security Design, **97**

Matisse, Henri: *The Windshield, On the Road to Villacoublay*, 30

Matthias Megyeri, Germany, **100** (see also Megyeri, Matthias)

Mayne, Desmond: EVAC+ Emergency Escape Smoke Hood, **165**

Médecins Sans Frontières (Doctors Without Borders): Bracelet of Life, Middle Upper Arm Circumference (MUAC) measuring device, **180**

Med-Eng Systems, Inc., Canada: CHP 100 Conical Hand Protector, **88**

Med-Eng Systems Inc., Canada, **88, 203**

Megyeri, Matthias: Billy B. Old English Padlock, **102**; Heart to Heart chain, **102**; Landscape, **101**; Mr. Smish & Madame Buttly Razor Wire, **101**; Peter Pin, R. Bunnit, and Didoo Railings, **100**

Meier, Giovanni: Lifeline AED Semiautomatic External Defibrillator, **152**

Meier, Kim: How to Disappear kit and vending machine, **78**

Meiko Co., Ltd., Japan, **142**

Melin, Sigurd: NOAQ Tubewall Flood Fighting System, **163**

Mertens, Carl: Oyster Glove chain mail glove, **88**

Metaal 2000 BV, The Netherlands, **94**

Metaphase Design Group, Inc., USA: Solo Traveler Plus hot cup lid, **144**

MTA New York City Transit Team, USA, **187**

Meza, Marco: Con Edison Cast Iron Covers, Type Q-8-VI, for Electric Manholes, **95**

Michael Rakowitz, USA, **68** (see also Rakowitz, Michael)

Million, Philippe: Barrier Bench, **98**

Mir, Ana: Kleensex disposable pocket sheet, **91**; Hot Box, **199**

MIT Media Lab, USA, **175**

Möbel-Transport AG, Switzerland, **119**

Möbel-Transport shipping company: logo, **119**

Moeslinger, Sigi: Bloomberg bUNIT Personal Authentication Device, **116**; Help Point Intercom for the New York City Subway, **187**

Mohss, Anders: NOAQ Tubewall Flood Fighting System, **163**

Mommy's Helper company design: Panda Door Pinch Guard, **125**

Mommy's Helper, Inc., USA, **125**

Mortensen, Peter: Life-Saving Station, **177**

Mulder, John: Mojo Barrier, **94**

Mulder, Roelf: Condom Applicator, **93**; FPR2 Human Powered Radio, **173**

Murase, Miwako: Fresh Kiss Breath Checker, **146**

Museum of Safety Gear for Small Animals, Canada, **158**

n

Naimanan, Khashayar: ça ne vaut pas un clou, **110**; Incognito dinnerware, **111**

Nanwa Co., Ltd., Japan, **81**

Nasco, USA, **186**

Nederlandse Vereniging voor een Vrijwillig Levenseinde, The Netherlands: Do Not Resuscitate Necklace, **117**

Neo Human Toys, The Netherlands, **74**

NEOS, New England Overshoe Company, Inc., USA, **90**

Neptunic Sharksuits, USA, **83**

NOAQ Flood Protection AB, Sweden, **163**

Noble, Terry: One-Day-At-A-Time Weekly Medication Organizer Tray, **181**

North Design, UK: Guide to the Flood Warning Codes, **194**

North Safety Products Development and Manufacturing Team, USA: Silver Shield/4H Chemical-Resistant Booties, **89**; Static Dissipative Finger Cots, **89**

North Safety Products, USA, **88, 89**

Noy, Thomas E.: Yaktrax Walker, **170**

Nymphenburg Porzellan-Manufaktur, Germany, **111**

o

OFFECCT, Sweden, **137**

Oh, Seunghee: China Telecom Kid Mobile Phone, **187**

Oliver, Andrew, II: GIANTmicrobes, **147**

Oliver, Joanne: Crave Aid satiety patches, **130**

O'Mara, Sean: "Keep Your Bag Safe!" Flyer, **106**

Opie, Steve: Industrial Overshoe/TPU12, **90**

Oroza, Ernesto: *Garden gate made from a refrigerator grille, Gibara, Cuba,* **14**

Orta, Lucy: Refuge Wear Habitent, **11**; Refuge Wear Intervention (frontispiece)

Osaka Senden Kenkyusho Co., Ltd.: ABOBA Blood Type Condoms, **92**

Overthun, Thomas: Crave Aid satiety patches, **130**

Øxseth, Hilde Angelfoss: Stokke Xplory baby stroller, **126**

Ozolins, Helmars: Bloomberg bUNIT Personal Authentication Device, **116**

p

Padrós, Emili: Hot Box, **199**

Park, Sungmee: Georgia Tech Wearable Motherboard, **179**

Pascoe, Vernon: 3-in-1 Inflatable Kite/Splint/Body Warmer, **156**

Patton, James: Corporate Fallout Detector, **175**

Pennsylvania State University, USA, **178**

Pentel Co., Ltd., Japan, **136**

Perez, Richard: Condom Applicator, **93**

Petzl International, France: Petzl catalogue of climbing equipment, **190**

Peyricot, Olivier: Vigilhome, **65**; Body Props, **127**

Philips Design, The Netherlands, **186**

Philips Medical Systems, The Netherlands, **152**

Pininfarina company design, Italy: Nido, **120**

Pinpon, France, **121**

Piper, Jackie: Stop Thief! Bentwood Chair Clone, **105**; Stop Thief! Ply Chair, **104**

Plawner, Marc: Personal SafetyVest, **164**

Pollen Design, USA , **164**

Poulsen, Anne Mette Karsted: How to Disappear kit and vending machine, **78**

Prada Beauty, Italy, **130**

Prestige Products, USA, **150**

Puma, Germany, **103**

q

Qingdao Gyoha Plastics Co., Ltd., China, **59**

Qually, Byron: Condom Applicator, **93**; FPR2 Human Powered Radio, **173**

r

Raby, Fiona: Electro-draught Excluder, **72**; Faraday Chair, **73**; Hide Away Furniture, **72**; Priscila Huggable Atomic Mushroom, **8**

Raikamo, Hedi: Zone One and Two, **107**

Rainer, Anna: Undercover Table, **161**

Rajamanickam, Rangaswamy: Georgia Tech Wearable Motherboard, **179**

Rakowitz, Michael: *paraSITE* homeless shelter, **68**

Ramsey, Richard: NoGo Barrier New York Financial District Streetscape and Security Design, **97**

Rashid, Karim: Monodose Skincare Cosmetics, **130**; Safe band-aids, **129**

RedStart Design, LLC, USA, **112**

Reeder, Frederick Arlen: Monolith, Tripart, and Oobelisk, Security Bollards, **97**

Refsum, Bjørn: Stokke Xplory baby stroller, **126**

Richardson, Chris: SPLICE low-cost land-mine detector, **201**

Rijkheer, Etienne: FPR2 Human Powered Radio, **173**

Rival swimwear, Australia: Ultraviolet protective swimwear, **44**

Robb, Hill Jephson: Cries and Whispers, **75**

Rocheleau Tool & Die Co. Inc., USA, **133**

Rogers Marvel Architects, PLLC, USA, **97**

Rogers, Robert: NoGo Barrier New York Financial District Streetscape and Security Design, **97**

Roke Manor Research, Ltd., UK, **201**

Rosburg, Klaus: Target ClearRx prescription system, **182**

Rosen, Mark: Inflate-A-Shield CPR Barrier, **153**

Rosenfeld, Galya: Headscarf, **82**

Rosenkrans, Louise: How to Disappear kit and vending machine, **78**

Rossignol, France, **14**

Royal College of Art, UK, **66**

Ruiz de Azúa, Martín: Basic House, **69**

Rutter, Bryce G.: Solo Traveler Plus re-closable hot cup lid, **144**

Ruyant, Frédéric: First-Aid Bag for the French Red Cross, **151**

Ryden, Derek: Blizzard Survival Bag, **157**

s

Sables, Jonathan: FreeCharge Mobile Phone Charger, **172**

Saez, Manuel: Personal SafetyVest, **164**

Sam Medical Products, USA, **155**

SARS mask, **14**

Satellite du Musée d'Art Moderne de Paris, France, **65**

Scheinberg, Sam: SAM Finger Splint, **155**

Schiebel Elektronische Geraete GmbH, Austria, 200, **202**

Seeley, Damon: Urban Nomad Shelter inflatable homeless shelter, **67**

Sener, Jim: Lifeline AED Semi-automatic External Defibrillator, **152**

Sen Tech BioMed Corporation, USA, **178**

Serbinski, Andrew: Inflate-A-Shield CPR Barrier, **153**

Setco, Inc., USA, **182**

Shalon, Ltd., Israel, **168**

Shanxi Yuansheng Industrial Co., China, **95**

Shapla Water Products, Bangladesh, **141**

Shaughnessy, Sara: Subtle Safety Defensive Ring, **112**

Shigeru Ban Architects, Japan, **61** (see also Ban, Shigeru)

Shimizu, Kazuhisa: B Threwny Static Electricity Remover, **136**

Shimizu, Takeshi: Kuroneko (black cat) logo for Yamato Transport Co., Ltd, **119**

Shoji, Tamaki: Fresh Kiss Breath Checker, **146**

Siemens Transportation Systems, USA, **187**

Sinclair, Iain: Flashcard, **197**

Sinclair Rush, USA, **150**

Skibsted, Jens Martin: Puma Bike, **103**

Skovmand, Ole: PermaNet 2.0 Long Lasting Insecticidal Mosquito Net, **62**; Zerofly Plastic Sheeting with Incorporated Insecticide, **62**

Skystreme UK, Ltd., UK, **156**

Snowcrash AB, Sweden, **137**

Solo Cup Company, USA, **144**

Søndergaard, Jan: Design for a Mobile HIV/AIDS Health Clinic, **46**

Sorensen, Jay D.: Java Jacket Cup Sleeve, **144**

SO WORKS Site Objects for Perimeter Force Protection, USA, **97**

Spiewak, USA: Jacket of 3M Scotchlite material, **41**

Ståhlbom, Mattias: Ballistic Assault Alarm Cell-Phone Charm, **114**

Startloop AS, Norway, **171**

Stokke AS, Norway, **126**

Stremple, Paul R.: BananaBunker, **133**

S.T. Safety Technologies, Israel, **168**

Student, Jörg: Ha-Ori Shelter, **66**

Sukcharoun, Sang: Neptunic C Sharksuit, **83**

Sullivan, Jeremiah: Neptunic C Sharksuit, **83**

Superweld, Ltd., Israel, **168**

Suruga Co., Ltd., Japan, **143**

Suruga company design: Patapata Pen Chan water running warning, **143**

Swaine, Michael: Homeland Security Blanket, **71**

Swann, John: EVAC+ Emergency Escape Smoke Hood, **165**

t

TAF Arkitektkontor AB, Sweden, **114**

Takahashi, Yasushi: Otohime YES300D artificial sound machine for the bathroom, **76**

Takara Co., Ltd., Japan, **124**

Takata Corporation, Japan, **121**

Tanita Corporation, Japan, **146**

Tarazi, Ezri: Bazooka Joe, **166**

Tazawa, Hiroyuki: Rescue Board 600, **154**; Snow Grabber, **170**

Theriault, Vicki: EVAC+ Emergency Escape Smoke Hood, **165**

Thomas, Chris: "Keep Your Bag Safe!" Flyer, **106**

Thomas, Mike: BaXstrap Spineboard, **155**

Thomson, Gregg: MultiCam Multi-Environment Camouflage, **77**

Thorpe, Adam: Karryfront Screamer bag, **108**; Phonesafe, **109**; Puma Bike, **103**; Scroll Top Backpack, **108**; See and Be Seen (SABS) Parka, **198**

3M company design: Class 95 Particulate Respirator, **135**; Inflata-Pak Air Cushion Packaging, **132**

3M, USA, **132, 135**

Tomozy, Eskil: Tylenol Bottle Concept, **131**

Torchco Ltd., Ukm **197**

Torolab, Mexico, **176**

TOTO, Ltd., Japan, **76**

Trapinex Serigraphie-Offset, France, **180**

Traut, Jim: BaXstrap Spineboard, **155**; Inflate-A-Shield CPR Barrier, **153**

Treible, Paul: Personal SafetyVest, **164**

Tretorn: Lumber pro class 3 Safety Boot, **90**

Trovan Engineering Team: Trovan ID-100A Transponder, **116**

Trovan, Ltd., UK, **116**

Tsumura, Kosuke: Final Home 44-pocket parka, **70**; Final Home Bear, **70**

Turner, Duncan: Too Hot to Handle, **145**

u

Udagawa, Masamichi: Bloomberg bUNIT Personal Authentication Device, **116**; Help Point Intercom for the New York City Subway, **187**

UNICEF United Nations Children's Fund: Water container, **149**

United Nations High Commissioner for Refugees: UNHCR Plastic Sheeting, **59**

University of California Santa Cruz Health Promotion, USA, **192, 993**

U.S. Armor Corporation, USA, **81, 95**

USS Baxley freighter with "dazzle" camouflage, **42**

v

Vaisnys, Gintaras: Lifeline AED Semiautomatic External Defibrillator, **152**

Vanstone, Chris: PowerPizza, **106**

Verdonck, Frans: Hingeling, **74**

Verdonck, Twan: Hingeling, **74**; Tummy, **74**; zHumanoyd, **74**

Vestergaard Frandsen S.A., Switzerland, **62**

Vexed Generation Clothing, Ltd., UK, **198**

Vexed Generation, UK, **103, 108, 109, 198**

Viking Life-Saving Equipment, Denmark, **162**

Vittori, Arturo: Desert Seal, **64**

Vlieger & Vandam, The Netherlands, **113**

Vlieger, Carolien: Guardian Angel handbag, **113**

Vogler, Andreas: Desert Seal, **64**

Volvo, Sweden, **26**

w

Wagner, Jakob: DrägerMan PSS 500 Air Unit for firefighters, **153**

Wahlgren, Pontus: Hair Card, **115**; Crave Aid satiety patches, **130**

Waitzkin, Graeme: NoGo Barrier New York Financial District Streetscape and Security Design, **97**

Wapenaar, Dré: Treetents, **63**

Webster, David. Crave Aid satiety patches, **130**

Wetton, Barnabas: How to Disappear kit and vending machine, **78**; Sea Shelter, **162**

Weyerhaeuser, USA, **60**

Whitmill, Barry: FreeCharge Mobile Phone Charger, **172**

Wilkes, Elizabeth A.: Clean Call disposable telephone covers, **135**

Willcocks, Marcus: "Keep Your Bag Safe!" Flyer, **106**; Stop Thief! Bentwood Chair Clone, **105**; Stop Thief! Ply Chair, **104**

Wisser Verpackungen GmbH, Germany, **140**

Wong, Tobias: Ballistic Rose Brooch, **85**; Bulletproof Quilted Duvet, **85**

Wright, Howard: Storm All-Weather Safety Whistle, **186**

x

...XYZ Dot Dot Dot Ex Why Zed Design, Ltd., South Africa, **93, 173**

y

Yaktrax, Inc., USA, **170**

Yamamoto, Yasuyuki: mizu-Q Straw Water Purifier, **142**

Yamato Transport Co., Ltd., Japan, **119**

Yang, Jae Bong: Ufocap umbrella, **142**

Yuille, Paul: Sporran-Utan, **107**

z

Zelco Industries, Inc., USA, **109**

Zeller, Adele: ToteGuard, **109**

Zielonka CNC Dreh- und Frästechnik GmbH, Germany, **148**

Zielonka, Dirk: Smellkiller, **146**

Zorkendorfer, Rico: Seed Card, **115**

Zwahlen, Stefan: FreeCharge Mobile Phone Charger, **172**

216